The New York Times ON
THE SOPRANOS

INTRODUCTION BY
STEPHEN HOLDEN

AFTERWORD BY
STEPHEN J. CANNELL

WITH A SERIES ANALYSIS BY
J. MADISON DAVIS

ibooks
NEW YORK
WWW.IBOOKS.NET

DISTRIBUTED BY SIMON & SCHUSTER

CONTENTS

TONY SOPRANO, AMERICAN HERO

A FOREWORD BY
J. MADISON DAVIS

FORMER PRESIDENT,
THE INTERNATIONAL ASSOCIATION OF
CRIME WRITERS, NORTH AMERICA

As surreal and inconceivably horrible as the events of September 11 were, it was only a few days later that jokes directed at the perpetrators began circulating across the World Wide Web. Most weren't very funny, but among the most widely circulated was a captioned photograph called "We'll Do the Job" featuring the Sopranos. Tony, Christopher, Hesh, Paulie, Big Pussy, Silvio Dante, and Furio are standing in front of Satriale's looking grim. The caption reads: "Just tell us where bin-Laden is and fuhgedaboudit!"

That we would even imagine a bunch of gangsters like these as our avengers says a lot about Americans and the particular place *The Sopranos* occupies in our hearts.

When the unimaginable happens—as it did on September 11—time stops. The heart is frozen and breathing halts. In such moments, it seems as if the universe has been mercilessly and madly recreated. All that is predictable has been suspended. Everything we have believed and cherished has become irrelevant, obscure, and foolish. The airplane slices into the building. The *Challenger* explodes. Walter Cronkite grimly announces that President Kennedy has died. Those frozen moments are never forgotten. They scar us as surely and as permanently as a bullet or a knife.

Yet, breath returns. Like a staggered boxer clawing his way up the ropes, we grasp one, than another, trying to grip something familiar and solid in our numbed fingers. We find our legs, trying to understand what has happened and to make sense of it. We cast about frantically to find a means to deal with those moments. Anger swells in the throat, of course, accompanied by a ravenous appetite for revenge, but often, almost always, those first exhalations of the returning breath expel a joke. Did you hear the one about the Amtrak train that derailed in a turkey farm? How about the one in which David Koresh arrives at the Pearly Gates? Did you laugh at any of those Ethiopian jokes of a few years back? Deny it if you like. Somebody was chuckling. Despite the shame we may feel at getting amusement at something tragic, we frequently exorcise our worst nightmares by laughing at them.

The *Sopranos* cartoon wasn't the only 9-11 joke, of course, but it was wildly popular and circulated from e-mail to e-mail because people thought it was funny and that their friends would find it funny as well. Other cartoons circulated. There were cheesy cartoons of Lady Liberty and Uncle Sam stomping on bin Laden, the Taliban, or various anonymous big-nosed Al Qaeda terrorists, but these were often racist and more embarrassing than funny. Often they were so abstract or jingoistic that they couldn't really be amusing at all.

The visual joke on 9-11 that had perhaps the widest circulation was an animation called the "Bin Laden Bomb Song" with lyrics by the morning show team at KOMP-FM, Las Vegas. The web site offering it, Got Laughs.com, accumulated millions of hits around the world, and the song was played on over 100 radio stations. In this Monty-Pythonesque collage of head photos on a cartoon background, Colin Powell sings to the tune of "The Banana Boat Song," the old Harry Belafonte hit, while a beady-eyed George Dubya—looking like he's just awakened after a long frat party at Yale—beats conga drums in the background. As Powell intones such lyrics as "Daylight come and I drop de bomb!" cruise missiles chase a bouncing bin Laden across a wasteland labeled "You Know Where" until a chunk is blown out of the planet. Since the animation begins with a view of the Earth from space, it implies a comment about the nature of life here on the blue marble, and the final shot of the chunk flying off into space might be seen as an ironic warning about the unpredictable consequences of making war. Belafonte himself was not amused, saying he was appalled by the D.J.'s trivializing a tragedy, but declined to sue.

It is interesting to note that the song said that Colin Powell, not Bush, was going to get bin Laden, and that Dubya was reduced to the role of backup singer. The positive response to all that says a lot about how the public felt about these two men, at least initially. As Jay Leno has remarked, a comedian cannot make a successful joke about something the public doesn't already believe. Later, when confidence in Dubya grew, many not as funny cartoons appeared with the president as a Western hero, striding into a gunfight or lasso-ing mullahs. But these all seemed kind of forced. Dubya's image has never seemed as threatening as Tony Soprano's, or as competent as Powell's. Dubya's brief military experience consisted of guarding Alabama from the Viet Cong air force and didn't exactly live up to his dad's heroism in the Big One. However, what's most interesting when we compare this Got Laughs animation to the Sopranos cartoon is that Colin Powell, the Mr. Clean of our time, takes roughly the same role in our comic fantasies that Tony Soprano occupies in the "fuhgeddaboutit" cartoon. Is our Secretary of State equivalent to a New Jersey payback artist? Or has Tony Soprano started wearing John Wayne's boots?

Certainly part of it comes from our sense that revenge is a dirty business and we need to send a man fit for that business. Colin Powell is our most respected living military man, who helped direct one of the most lopsided wars in history. We trust Powell to righteously kick some butt most righteously. Tony is a fictional being, of course, but there's no doubt that Tony knows revenge and he knows the uses of violence. Americans, despite frequently mouthing the cliché that they're peace-loving, are, as a whole, a violent people in a great many ways. We do believe that violence solves problems, or at least we fantasize it does, whether it consists of spanking an unruly child, decking the asshole who's flirting with your wife, or frying a serial killer. Turning the other cheek is an ideal we rarely live up to and usually consider naïve. We're all aware that in our society there are people who have made a science of violence, and we admire them, despite the half-hearted wish that we didn't. Why else is the action-adventure film Hollywood's bread and butter? Are Steven Seagal and Chuck Norris known for the delivery of their lines, the cleverness of their plots, or the sensitivity of their portrayals? We know that, judiciously employed, the masters of real violence can be very useful. Let's hear it for the 101st Airborne, swat teams, the French Foreign Legion, the Green Berets, and so on.

An efficient, immediate ending to the "war" on terrorism was what everyone wanted after 9-11: quick revenge. In the pause before the bombing of Afghanistan began, I heard a number of people ask the rhetorical question, "Isn't it time we killed some people?" We were losing patience while the Pentagon assembled its forces and the State Department gathered our allies. Go get them, we were saying. Finish it. Whack the bad guys and bury the pieces in the Pine Barrens. Drop them into the same black hole of a sausage grinder that digested Richie Aprile.

Perhaps you *do* need a mongoose to kill a snake, but that observation contrasts with a different aspect of Tony's persona: his essential lovability. John Wayne didn't get to be an American icon merely by breaking up dozens of saloons and mowing down unshaven outlaws. We liked the way he cocked his head and smiled wryly. We liked his way of saying "Pilgrim." Tony Soprano hasn't captured millions of imaginations merely because he gives great garrot. Critics write about America's fascination with the gangster, but still wonder at the amazing way *The Sopranos* gathered multitudes of subscribers for

HBO. Without thinking about it very much, knee-jerk critics and programmers at more restricted networks ascribed the success to the public's lust for sex and violence (Oh, woe to civilization!), despite the fact that the entertainment graveyard is filled with thousands of trashy movies and shows that had nothing to offer *but* sex and violence. David Caruso's buttocks didn't make a long-running hit out of *NYPD Blue*—his buttocks left the show very quickly, in fact—and there is little on cable that is more boring than those soft-core hump movies that run at night on HBO's sister network Cinemax, or the throat-ripping, blood-gushing fare we used to think was only for drive-ins. Besides the fact this stuff never comes across as realistic anyway, it is silly to argue that merely sex and violence is the primary reason for the success of *The Sopranos*.

The Sopranos manages something much more difficult to do with an explicitly bad gangster character than merely promote sex or violence in a misguided attempt to "tell it like it is." As Raymond Chandler wrote in his great essay "The Simple Art of Murder," nothing is duller than a goaty young man writing about dalliances with promiscuous blondes only because he's interested in dalliances with promiscuous blondes. But even if the sex and violence is authentic to the circumstances of the story, realism isn't quite enough, says Chandler. In every successful story there must be some sense of redemption. Nobody thinks of Al Pacino's Michael Corleone in *The Godfather* as "lovable"—or as a sexy "teddy bear," but more than one fan posting has described Tony that way—to James Gandolfini's great surprise. Corleone is sexy, but in an invulnerable way. Tony gives off a more human feel, and because of that, in our heart of hearts, whether we admit it or not, we *like* Tony Soprano. Maybe we don't approve of the things he does, but we still like him. Maybe we don't really understand his behavior in many respects, but we nonetheless like him. Maybe we really despise his lifestyle, his philandering, his language, his violence. Most of us are about as capable of dealing with violence as the peasant farmers in *The Seven Samurai* or *The Magnificent Seven*. We're helpless and would be quite happy to hire unemployed warriors to protect us. On the other hand, we don't want them influencing our children, dating our daughters, or hanging around the kitchen. Rudyard Kipling summarized the attitude in his poem about British soldiers (Tommy's):

> For it's Tommy this, an' Tommy that, an'
> "Chuck him out, the brute!"
> But it's "Saviour of 'is country"
> when the guns begin to shoot.

We only like our violent men when they have a job to do. We often don't like what they do in order to do the job, but we like sending them off to do it with three hurrahs and ten thousand flags.

Of course, Tony could care less what most people think about anything he does. Who da hell are *you*? He'd tell you what you could do with your f**king attitude. You surely wouldn't want a guy like Tony at your dinner table or living in your suburb, would you? And yet, you'll sign up for HBO, just so—as they used to say on old television, you can invite Tony into your living rooms. No, there's more to Tony's being an imaginary representative of America against Osama bin Laden than his ability to send guys to the fishes. The affection he draws is much deeper.

A part of Tony's appeal lies in the fact that he has a kind of unlimited freedom which we all fantasize. You can bet that most of the men watching Tony's access to an assortment of mistresses or girls from the Badda-Bing Club take a moment to imagine what *that* would be like, and the fantasy of operating outside the law is a powerful one. In the recent remake of *Bedazzled*, Elliott (Brendan Fraser) asks the Devil (Elizabeth Hurley) for money and power. To his horror he is transformed into a Columbian drug lord, which, whether we like it or not, is certainly one of the most powerful and lucrative jobs in the world. We like to tell ourselves we're a nation of laws, yet we chafe at the restrictions which any system of laws imposes, particularly when the rule of law seems to operate contrary to our sense of justice. It doesn't take much to get into a conversation in which someone begins to rant about defendants' rights, the absurdity of the criminal justice system, and how criminals are set free to do evil again. The *Death Wish* movies, in which Charles Bronson mowed down a baker's dozen of malefactors, sold a lot of tickets, even after they had lost all their credibility in four repetitive sequels. In the first film, the hero was avenging the murder of his wife and rape of his daughter. After that he was just street-cleaning any vermin he encountered—and he found them with little difficulty.

"Go ahead. Make my day," was borrowed cheerfully from *Dirty Harry* by no less than the president and still reverberates in its joyful liberation of justice from strict legality. *Dirty Harry* also begat four sequels, which, though less lamentable than *Death Wish* sequels, lacked the startling edge of the original. As you'll recall, the bad guy (played by Andrew Robinson) kills a girl and gets away with it because Harry Callahan (Clint Eastwood) oversteps his legal rights as a policeman. Harry tortures the guy to find out where the victim has been buried underground, but when rescue workers reach the girl, her oxygen bottle has already run out and she has suffocated. Since torture was used, the villain is set free by the courts to do evil again. Later, after Callahan corners him, there is none of that usual movie nattering about how shooting the bad guy would make Harry the immoral equivalent of the kidnapper. There's none of that hooey in which an overwrought avenger is persuaded to put down his gun by the second banana cop, sheriff, boyfriend, or other character. The "most powerful handgun in the world" ventilates the bad guy's innards, the credits roll, and the audience cheers. Dead guys don't manipulate juries or earn reversals in the court of appeals. End of story.

While Dirty Harry gets his freedom by tiptoeing along the edges of legal boundaries, he maintains a certain boundary at times—he doesn't fire until he tempts the punk to go for the gun. That's perhaps a movie morality concession to the audience. Harry is a policeman, after all, and the movie was criticized enough for its message without going as far as *Death Wish*. Tony Soprano, on the other hand, dances like a great bear far outside any lines not of his own making. In the Season 1 episode "Boca," Tony and his gang try to persuade April Soprano's soccer coach, Don Hauser, not to leave town to take another job. They ply him with a large screen television and other persuasions, which he insultingly rejects. Tony then discovers that Hauser has molested Ally Vandermeer, one of the girls he coaches. Faced with such a discovery, most of us in the real world would want to pound the bastard into marinara, but we'd know we couldn't. We'd have to persuade the victim to testify and hope that she didn't trip over her words or look like an underage temptress to a skeptical judge and jury, and pray that the rapist didn't end up with community service and a treatment program. If we couldn't get the victim to testify or the law to remove the molester from our community, we might be left with ostracizing him and making sure he never got anywhere near our own kids.

Tony, however, is capable of making vermin disappear from the universe by exchanging a few quiet words with Paulie and Christopher. The fact that he doesn't, doesn't come from a realization he couldn't. Whatever scruples he has are not inspired by a respect for the law. When Artie Bucco begs him to leave it to the law and asks him what good it will do for the victim or anyone to take revenge, Tony throws him out, saying all that will happen with the legal system is that Hauser will get two years in jail, move to Saskatchewan and molest someone else's little girl. Tony has no illusions about the law's effectiveness. The law doesn't exist in Tony's world, except as a nuisance that interferes with his business and, ironically, as a means to do business. How could the various Mafias exist if it wasn't for people who ordinarily obey the law, going to the gangs for illegal substances and services? Tony is not the only Mafioso who has rationalized his sources of income in this way and considered himself a "simple businessman." The fact that Tony decides, in a brilliantly written plot twist, to leave the molester to the legal system only underscores the completeness of Tony's freedom. Violence is a genuine option for him, a very appealing option, the most obvious and effective option, but he rolls around the floor in great drunken delight in his recognition that he does not have to choose it.

It's interesting to compare this to the Season 3 episode "Employee of the Month," in which Dr. Melfi is raped. She recognizes that she holds a great power: Tony is the snarling dog of her dreams. All she has to do is say, "Sic!" and the dog will ruthlessly avenge her violation. He'll rip out the creep's throat, then calmly drop by Artie Bucco's for a plate of scongole. The fact that she can do this, speak a few words to Tony and inflict as much pain on her assailant as she wants, helps her adjust to the trauma of the rape. The criminal justice system fails her miserably and doesn't seem to care about its failure. Always disturbed by the association between the

Italian-American community and organized crime, she is tempted to embrace what she has tried so hard to avoid, that "thing" of certain Sicilians, their justice outside the law. In the end, however, it is enough for her to know that she has this freedom to choose revenge. When Tony asks her if there is something she wants to tell him, she says only, "No." In the end, she cannot continue to be Dr. Jennifer Melfi, psychiatrist, by living outside the law. Choosing not to unleash Tony—something most viewers would have found, if not exhilarating, understandable—reinforced her conception of herself as having risen above those few Italian-Americans who were tempted into a life of crime. She chooses the law with its failings over invalidating the law by seeking Cosa Nostra justice. The implication of Tony's choice not to hurt the child molester is slightly different: he is not asserting his assimilation into society; he is relishing the options of being outside it. He laughs and remarks how funny it is to him that he hasn't hurt somebody.

Entertainment gives us dozens of fantasies of freedom. The Marx Brothers attend a dinner party with stuffed shirts and end up running on top of the banquet table. Groucho compares a Chair of History to part of a dining room set. Harpo sees a pretty girl and without hesitation chases her up and down corridors. It wouldn't be funny if some part of us didn't want to do the same things in similar situations. The courage to throw a pie at a pompous ass is something most of us can only daydream, but, oh, what a pleasure it would be! On the serious side of freedom, Americans imagine the open spaces of the wilderness, riding horseback across an open prairie, sleeping under the stars, hunting our own meals, going where the weather suits our clothes. One theory about why handyman's books sell so well is because men read them, imagining the kind of self-sufficiency they cannot manage in their real lives. How many basements have elaborate woodworking machines gathering dust? Retirees buy themselves enormous motor homes, take a trip or two, then return to the comfort of their La-Z-Boys. It has been reported several times that the number one rental among taped books is Henry David Thoreau's *Walden*. Commuters, sealed in their cars, dawdling along in traffic jams, consider their lives of quiet desperation and imagine what it would be like to flee the world of commerce, build a cabin in the woods, and live off the land. Easy rider! Born to be wild! Don't fence me in!

It's a very American fantasy. In a BBC documentary, Japanese fans of *Bonanza* were interviewed in a country and western bar in Tokyo. Asked what they liked about the show, they admired how the people on the frontier worked together for the common good. Undoubtedly a similar view of the Sopranos would come from that culture, emphasizing the "taking care of the family" rationalizations that Mafiosi have long used: Carmela's sacrifices, Tony's worries about his kids and his promises to Jackie Aprile to take care of his son. Americans, on the other hand, tend to see the Cartwrights on the Ponderosa as a family standing alone against man and nature. They would emphasize Carmela's courage and Tony's power to lead.

Most Westerns and private eye novels show us something even more extreme, an individual against all. The townspeople having abandoned him, Marshall Will Kane waits for the train in *High Noon*. Walking down those mean streets in *Farewell, My Lovely*, Philip Marlowe must take on the police and the mob to get anything that resembles justice. The rugged, independent individual may be our cherished fantasy but, on the other hand, it is not necessarily a sensible one, and we know it. It's worth a news story when a stockbroker chucks his job on Wall Street to become a bush pilot in the Yukon. Most of those desperate commuters frustrated by the freeways wouldn't do any better living off the land than the hundreds of early colonists who died in misery at Jamestown and Roanoke. (Or Paulie and Christopher lost in the Pine Barrens!) Nature doesn't offer central heat or air conditioning and features an amazing variety of crawling things, many of which bite. Independence is a tough gig. It takes *stugats* and it takes skill. Tony, in his two-story cabin in the wilds of New Jersey, has got both.

If we compare Tony to Michael Corleone again, we see a much different situation. When Corleone returns to his family after having fought in World War II, he is an all-American vet who's done his duty for god and country. He doesn't have the kind of background that Tony has. His mother is saintly and her goodness has manifested itself in him. Because of this, his family has no intention to bring him into the role he eventually acquires. He doesn't seem suited for it and he is offered the chance to leave it behind. As the story evolves, however, Vito is nearly fatally wounded and Sonny (who wouldn't have had the brains to be an effective *capo di tutti capi*) is murdered. Michael begins to assume his destiny to be leader. *The Godfather* is the story of how Michael Corleone comes to maturity and accepts his role as the head of the family. It is an ironic coming of age story, essentially the story of a boy becoming his father, or that of a weakling or insignificant prince who rises to become the best sort of king, as Prince Hal does in Shakespeare's Henry plays, or Arthur does in the legends. This underlying structure is an important element in giving *The Godfather* its epic feel.

Yet, Michael Corleone is more a mythic character than Tony Soprano is. Faced with a number of painful choices, such as what to do about his dimwitted brother Fredo's betrayal, Michael elects to accept the obligations which being a godfather require. There is the sense that if he chooses to ignore those obligations, he will have repudiated his right to be the godfather. It would be as if Arthur had plucked the sword from the stone, proving he is the "rightwise king of England," and then refused the crown. When Shakespeare's King Lear decides that it would be much more comfortable to retire and let someone else run the government, the entire kingdom falls apart. The implication is that when you're a king, you either act like a king or everyone suffers. Similarly, Michael must either act like a godfather or the Corleones will lose all that Vito built for them. In that sense, Michael has no freedom. He couldn't really let Fredo live and be an effective godfather, no matter how much it hurts him to have him killed. Michael's story is about accepting his destiny. He's heroic for having sacrificed himself to his fate.

No matter how much Tony admires *The Godfather* and would like to model himself on Vito and Michael Corleone, Tony's story is that of a man who has no destiny. There is no externally imposed order for him. Tony is more of a modern man caught in a meaningless universe, making his choices in order to create what resembles a destiny, but which never really is. This is not to say there are no consequences to his actions. Everything he does has consequence. However, there is little sense of an external structure that he must live up to. All of the Soprano gangsters and family members have a nostalgia, as it were, for the order they see in *The Godfather*, parts I and II (And whatever happened in part III?, as Carmela asked in exasperation). Tony is not trying to fit into a preconceived order, but struggling with trying to create an order. Tony is condemned to freedom, and that reality seems more like our day-to-day situation than the heroic milieu in which Michael Corleone operates.

My critical ink has flowed in trying to explain the appeal of the gangster in American entertainment. Antiheroes have shown up in fiction and poetry for some time, and movies found buckets of profits in using gangsters as antiheroes. However, the antihero is not a staple of television fare and has tended to avoid making gangsters the central character of any series. Stories set in the gangster world have been popular on television, but the premise usually revolves around a gangster who is not a gangster, someone who is an undercover agent. A lot of the interest revolved around a gangster character for whom the undercover guy could develop affection, but still be obligated to destroy. Often, the gangster could be a more interesting character than the undercover agent, but the premise was always that when the chips were down, the good guy would suppress his affection for the bad guy and send him to the Big House. *Wiseguy*, for example, features Ken Wahl in the role of Vinnie Terranova, who has deeply infiltrated the mob. Sonny Steelgrave, played by Ray Sharkey, was much more interesting than Terranova. In another notable example, *Crime Story*, policeman Michael Torello (Dennis Farina) week after week went after Ray Luca, a rising gangster in the 1950s, who was played with style by Anthony Denison. The word "chemistry" was often used to describe the relationship between Torello and Luca. It has to play that way because we have to see what attracts the good guy to the bad, so that we see that the protagonist has sorrow in bringing down someone who's become his friend. Otherwise we might think too much about the undercover guy's cold deception. It's not that emotionally different from what happens between Sam Spade and Brigid O'Shaughnessy in *The Maltese Falcon*. Spade genuinely loves her, but cannot be Spade without doing something about the person who killed his partner.

Among the most successful series about gangsters was *The Untouchables*, which began in April

1959 as a special two-part episode of *Desilu Playhouse*. About the fall of Al Capone, it was such a hit that it became a series that fall. It was still popular when it lost its sponsors, primarily Chesterfield cigarettes, which were reacting to pressure from groups that felt Italian-Americans were being defamed by it. (Ironically, one later group, the Italian Anti-Defamation League, was founded in 1970 by Joseph Colombo, head of the Profaci family.) The Italian aspects of the Mafia in American were played down, using villains such as Miles O'Banion and Dutch Schultz and even Nazis. It was also—do things ever really change?—accused of exploiting violence and being far too gritty for television. The violence was suppressed as well and they tried to emphasize Eliot Ness's "human side." All this meant that it had drifted away from the documentary style which had made it interesting in the first place and the ratings slipped somewhat. This allowed the network to get out from under the controversy and the show went off the air in 1963.

Ness, played by Robert Stack, was a steady character who weekly brought down one gangster after another—jokingly referred to as the "goombah of the week." Most of the interest was in the characters of the gangsters: Capone, Mad Dog Coll, Frank Nitty (who became a kind of arch-villain whose underlings Ness would round up while Nitty escaped). But no matter how interesting the gang-ster appeared in *The Untouchables,* particularly in contrast to the grim-voiced Ness, the criminal always remained the antagonist rather than the pro-tagonist. Television has consistently been oversen-sitive to the accusation that it is in some way undermining the foundations of our society, particu-larly when there were only the three networks. When Fox tried to shove its chair up to the network banquet table, it went out on a limb and took some heat for going too far with *Married, With Children* and Bart Simpson's language. Once at the table, Fox began to worry about the heat.

When David Chase first tried to sell his idea for *The Sopranos*, he discovered that ABC and Fox were jittery about the idea of leaving Tony Soprano an unmitigated gangster. They hinted they would be more comfortable if they could have Tony helping out the FBI, or something like that. That has been a staple of television almost from the beginning. "What do you do when you're branded?" as the old western theme song ran. Everybody in *Branded* thinks Lucas McCord (played by Chuck Connors) is a coward, but the audience knows he's not. The old-fashioned "bad guy who's really a good guy" that television has worked so many times didn't appeal to Chase. Everybody knows it's a cop-out intended to avoid the protests of our moral watchdogs. Chase ended up at HBO, whose original movies (*Conspiracy, Wit, Lumumba*) and series (*Sex and the City, Oz*) are often far beyond the pale of the usual commercial films and television series. When CBS attempted to respond to HBO's success with *The Sopranos*, the best they could come up with was *Falcone*, about an undercover agent infiltrating the mob.

Gangster movies in which the leading character is unquestionably bad have long been popular fare on the big screen and the portrayals by James Cagney, Edward G. Robinson, Humphrey Bogart, and others have become part of the shared culture, not just of America, but of the world. Cagney smashes the grapefruit into Mae Clark's face in *Public Enemy*. In *White Heat* he crows, "Made it, Ma! Top of the World!" *Little Caesar* ends with the famous line "Can this be the end of Rico?" Paul Muni laughs at murder in *Scarface*. Richard Widmark pushes the old lady down the stairs in *Kiss of Death*. "Mad Dog" Roy Earl is surrounded and shoots it out at the end of *High Sierra*. Martin Scorsese's three gangster films—*Goodfellas, Casino*, and *Mean Streets*—provide an often shocking harshness, but they have also provided several moments that have become part of our culture, such as when Joe Pesci attacks a man with a pen. The characters in all these films are often intriguing and their criminality is sometimes somewhat justified as the result of social forces: poverty, the Depression, injustice. The fact that Ida Lupino loves Roy Earl so much makes him much more human. When Pat O'Brien persuades Cagney to die like a coward in *Angels with Dirty Faces* so that children won't look up to him, you see a bit of redemption. But, on the whole, the message is very clear: *crime doesn't pay.* Gangsters are headed for a reckoning. Society might make criminals, but it isn't society that will get the electric chair, the gallows, or a gut full of lead. There hasn't been much different in that message since the 1930s, whether you're talking the remake of *Scarface, New Jack City, Blow,* or *Traffic.*

The latter is the most spectacular proof that Hollywood hasn't changed very much. *Traffic* spends most of its 147 minutes proving what an insurmountable problem the drug trade is, does a Tinkers-to-Evers-to-Chance triple play of Hollywood cop-outs to disprove it all as it concludes. Interweaving three plotlines made the film look more profound than it was, but each storyline was routine. The drug czar story with Michael Douglas—an opus of monumental silliness—ends with the stupidly optimistic view that holding hands with your daughter at a twelve-step program will take care of her addiction and prostitution. The undercover cop story featuring Benicio Del Toro (the best of the three stories) winds up with a rounding up of the drug lord and his crew and the implication that the future of Mexico will be supplying shortstops rather than cocaine. The third plotline is the inspiring story of how a drug lord's wife takes up the business and holds her family together when her husband is arrested—Could this lead to a series on Lifetime or Oxygen? They thought she was merely a trophy wife with silicone for brains! Plucky Helena Ayala (played by Catherine Zeta-Jones) saves the family business and many a farmer in the mountains of Columbia! But to avoid the criticism that Hollywood is glamorizing the drug trade, the cop played by Don Cheadle cleverly plants a bug in the Ayala's office, implying that the plucky mom we've been rooting for is going down. After the movie. Sometime in the future. Maybe. Drug lords never scan for bugs. That's why there are no rich drug lords. Shooting Scarface or Little Caesar or "Mad Dog" Earl full of more holes than are in a cheese grater may seem obviously moralistic now, but at least they had the good sense in 90-minute movies not to do it three times.

Maybe the movie studios—whether they know it or not—are incorporating Aristotle's warning that a play in which a bad guy prospers would be repugnant. However, we all sense where our interest lies through much of such films. It's Tom Powers played by James Cagney who provides all the interest in *The Public Enemy*, not his good brother Mike

Powers, played by Donald Cook. In *Angels with Dirty Faces* the Reverend Jerry Connolly (Pat O'Brien) demonstrates what you *should* do after growing up in the slums, but it's Rocky Sullivan (Cagney, again) who seems heroic at the end, sacrificing his own tough guy reputation to save the Dead End Kids—as if that were possible! "Mad Dog" Earl dies like a man. We feel sorry for Little Caesar and his pathetic death. We secretly admire Cody Jarrett in *White Heat*, the flames of the chemical plant lighting his face as he shouts, "Top of the world, Ma!" It's a Satanic image, yes, but let's not forget that Samuel Taylor Coleridge once argued that the real hero of John Milton's *Paradise Lost* is Lucifer, the most beautiful of angels, who won't submit to authority, who would rather rule in Hell than serve in Heaven. By contrast, God in Milton is all diffused light, golden thrones, and Muzac choirs. He's Milton's Rev. Jerry Connolly and it's *Paradise Lost* that is so much more vivid than its sequel, *Paradise Regained*. Similarly, it is Dante's *Inferno* is much more entertaining than his *Paradiso*. Perfection is too abstract. We all know imperfection and can more easily imagine and even fantasize being evil.

One of the things we admire about Tony Soprano is his self-awareness. The central element of the series from the beginning is his quest for self-discovery. Psychiatrists have regularly praised *The Sopranos* for having the most accurate representation of psychotherapy in a dramatic medium, and perhaps this contributes to our sense of a real human being. He knows he's a gangster, but there's a great deal he doesn't understand about himself. The ancient Greeks recommended "Know thyself," but we all know how difficult that is and how it becomes one of the primary psychic struggles. After Freud, alienated people became very serious about finding their "true selves," and whether this is merely a notion peculiarly intoxicating us in the twentieth century and hanging over to the twenty-first doesn't matter. Tony's interest in the question of who he is puts him a cut above many of the people around him. It makes him seem more intelligent and more like we wish ourselves to be in this respect.

If you compare him to his main rivals, there is a great contrast. Richie Aprile gets angry, reacts to that anger, and doesn't think. He cripples a good man, insists on what he imagines to be his rightful share when it makes no sense to do so, and clumsily engages in a plot against Tony. He should have been smart enough to know just a bit more about the woman he lived with. Ralph Cifaretto might be Richie's twin in this respect. He is knee-jerk violent. He lacks self-doubt. Like Richie, he seems destined for a fall simply because he will misjudge his own abilities and reach out too far. His surviving Season 3 is somewhat surprising, although the writers of the show may have been trying to avoid looking like they were "doing a Richie" all over again.

Tony's internal struggle to find his "self" is, like all our personal struggles, a tug of war against the received life. As mentioned earlier, Michael Corleone finds himself in accepting the received life. Tony, however, seem to have an anguish that the life he has been offered is not entirely real. Characters refer to the "tradition" of Italian-American gangsterism frequently throughout the series and it's obvious that members of the Mob try to live up to the Mafia traditions as represented in the mass media. *Honor Thy Father* by Gay Talese reported that Mafiosi were big fans of *The Untouchables*, and it has been alleged that a number of Mafia rituals were fabricated by Mario Puzo in writing *The Godfather*, transported into the movie, and then embraced as authentic rituals by real mobsters. FBI surveillance tapes have revealed that real-life New Jersey and New York mobsters are big fans of *The Sopranos*.

In the Season 3 episode "Proshai, Livuska," we see Tony watching *The Roaring Twenties* on television after his mother's funeral. He is trying to come to grips with his mother's death, obviously, and with the fact that she was quite memorably an irritation to the human species, but particularly to her family. Tony, Paulie, and all of them to varying degrees look for gangster role models and several of them become aware that reality is another country. Christopher finds his being "made" more than just a reward; it is hard work. Junior gets caught between the notion of how he ought to be respected and the fact that he is a master of oral sex, so he dumps the woman he loves. In Tony's case, however, the selection of *The Roaring Twenties* is quite significant, because there is such an Oedipal aspect to the Cagney character's relationship with his mother, an element which is reprised in *White Heat.* In the scene Tony watches, Tom Powers is dumped at the door in front of his brother, while Ma is upstairs happily getting his bed ready. Tony's mother was the anti-mother compared to Tom's, but *The Roaring Twenties* is an old black-and-white fantasy of the gangster world. Tony might want his mother to have been like Ma Powers, but, hey, he knows it was just a movie. The mothers of gangsters aren't like that. Are *any* mothers as faithful and unblinkingly loving as Ma?

We admire Tony because he tries to live up to a code, even if that code is a criminal one. We see few enough people in the world who really sacrifice anything personal for the sake of a code of behavior, and outright hypocrisy is the common coin of our lives, especially now that the mass media gleefully reports politicians' sexual predations and corporate executives defend their thievery with earnest faces. In one of the Season 1 episodes, Tony laments the fact that the young gangsters were no longer willing to have the "penal experience" to prevent testifying against their comrades in crime. In another episode, he forces Christopher to make up his mind and commit to him totally. He kills the squealer on the college trip with Meadow, but he also kills his friend Big Pussy for the same reason. He protects his family from harm.

Yet, we have the sense that he knows that he is like a father who slipped vodka into his Coke at high school football games, yet threatens his own children if he catches them doing the same. Tony does not want his soldiers to be involved with drugs, and yet he cannot be unaware that they are often stoned. How can anyone otherwise explain Christopher's strange monologue at the memorial service for Livia Soprano? Tony insists on enforcing certain rules in his gang, but does he believe in them? Or is the enforcement a way of maintaining order, a purely Machiavellian strategy similar to Henry IV of France deciding that Paris was well worth a mass? Tony received the code and is now burdened with enforcing the code. Why? Because he is the boss.

We see in Tony a guy who imagines a past time

of honor among thieves, of dignified gangsters. Yet the madeleine that reminds him of the past is capicolla. His father and Junior chop off a butcher's hand, and that memory induces a panic attack. We sense that Tony knows that he romanticizes the history of the Cosa Nostra, but out of nostalgia, he nonetheless longs to be part of that rationalization, to have the tradition be more than a fantasy. In the Paul Simon song, "Call Me Al," the narrator asks who will be his role model, now that his role models are gone. Who will be Tony's role model, if his role models never existed? Yes, we long for George Bush to be Franklin Delano Roosevelt, but we know he's not. What's more, we all know these days that FDR wasn't the FDR we want to imagine. It's a blessing that George Washington has remained somewhat of a mystery. He thereby becomes a projection screen for our deepest wishes. He becomes an ideal to live up to, even though we know in our hearts he probably couldn't live up to that ideal himself.

We can't help but like Tony Soprano. He suffers as we do. He has a freedom to act which most of us could never have—which is a good thing in a civilized nation. Yet, in his choices, he struggles to live up to an ideal he knows he cannot ever attain. Anyone who is self-aware knows this struggle and sympathizes with it. When Anthony Jr. reads the philosophers and begins to say life is meaningless,

Tony is furious. Why? Because he believes life is meaningful? No, he wants to protect his child from an awful truth, an awful truth he confronts every day. The ducks fly away and here we are. Here on this darkling plain, where ignorant armies clash by night, we know his loneliness.

THE SOPRANOS: AN INTRODUCTION

BY

STEPHEN HOLDEN

Early in 1999, as word began to spread that the Home Box Office series *The Sopranos* was not only the best television drama ever made, but episode by episode as good or better than any Hollywood movie to be released in ages, people who had never considered ordering a cable channel scrambled to subscribe to Home Box Office to see what the fuss was about.

What they discovered, along with millions who were already hooked on the series, was richly textured comic realism of a complexity and truthfulness that had never before been seen on television, not even in such beloved British series as *Upstairs Downstairs*, *Brideshead Revisited*, and *I, Claudius*.

The brainchild of writer-director David Chase, *The Sopranos* follows the fortunes of the

Sopranos, an upper-middle class New Jersey clan whose paterfamilias Tony Soprano just happens to be a local Mafia kingpin. The series deals head-on with questions about family, community, crime, and ethics that not even *The Godfather* films, which brought a new level of tragic realism to cinema in the 1970s, dared address.

The short answer to those questions, which are concerned with the integration of criminal life and a so-called "normal" life, is that it's not that big a deal. For *The Sopranos* subscribes unblinkingly to the absurd view of history, which is the version that most of us live by even if we don't know it. In the absurd view of life, it's people's little quirks and kinks that make big things happen. Modern wars and coups are just as likely to be the products of mood swings, temper tantrums, ruffled pride, and childish score-settling as the outcomes of ideological and spiritual crusades. After all, hasn't the world always had its share of Caligula-like despots who rule without rhyme or reason and sometimes destroy whole societies?

The Caligula-like despot in *The Sopranos* is Tony's widowed mother Livia, an ominous matriarch who subtly coerces her mobster brother-in-law Junior to take out a contract on Tony's life. Why would a mother do such a thing? Out of paranoia and spite, it turns out. She resents him for pressuring her to leave the home she is no longer able to manage and go live in a ritzy retirement home which he pays for, but which she believes to be a nursing home. On learning that Tony has been seeing a psychiatrist, Livia is seized with the outraged certainty that he spends his therapy sessions denouncing her.

Tony's uncle Junior, who orders the hit, is as believably crazy in his way as Livia is in hers. When his loyal longtime girlfriend boasts in a nail salon of Junior's prowess at performing oral sex, the news filters back to Tony, who mercilessly ribs Junior about bedroom etiquette that Tony and his macho cronies scorn as unmanly. Junior's humiliation and fury seriously deepens the potentially murderous breach between uncle and nephew.

Over the course of the series hour-long episodes, these and other wounds accumulate the force of Greek tragedy. Or is it a Chekhov comedy replayed in the foul-mouthed street language of New Jersey hoodlums? For if *The Sopranos* is often laugh-out-loud funny, the laughter it elicits doesn't come from one-liners but from a deeper recognition of the screaming little baby inside every grownup.

The Sopranos, more than any American television show, looks, feels and sounds like real life as it's lived in the United States in the cluttered environment of the Internet, mall shopping, rap music and a runaway stock market. Watch any episode and you're likely to come away with the queasy feeling of consuming a greasy slice of here and now with its surreal mixture of prosperity and brutishness. Tony's New Jersey mob boss isn't an exotic evil king holed up in a fortified stone castle. He is a harried forty-something middle-class Joe who, except for his occupation, is not all that different from the rest of us.

The Sopranos sustains its hyper-realism with an eye and ear so exquisitely attuned to contemporary culture and social niceties that it just might be the greatest work of American popular culture of the last quarter century. It was in 1974 that the second of *The Godfather* movies was released. Together with its 1971 forerunner, it gave American culture a new myth, inspired by the 20th century immigrant experience to replace the old one of the frontier and the winning of the west. *The Sopranos* carries *The Godfather* movies' epic vision into the present, turning tragedy into comedy and vice versa.

The series' greatness lies in its creation of at least a dozen indelible characters whom we come to know as intimately as close friends. At the center looms James Gandolfini's Tony, a hairy-shouldered grizzly bear who loves his wife Carmela and teenage children (the obedient Meadow and the rowdy Tony, Jr.), who watches the History Channel and blows off steam by pumping iron in the basement of his New Jersey home. Out of the blue one day, Tony starts suffering devastating panic attacks. When it's discovered there's nothing physically wrong with him, he begins to see Dr. Jennifer Melfi (Lorraine Bracco), a local psychiatrist recommended by the doctor who lives next door.

There are two essentially two Tonys. One is a mobster involved in theft, loan-sharking, drugs, and corrupt unions. This Tony takes brutal relish in beating up and killing those who cross him. The other Tony is a strait-laced family man who frets that his two children have discovered he isn't really in "waste management" as he claims. This is the same Tony who flares up when his daughter brings up sex at the dinner table and announces that in his house it is still 1954. Yet this devoted family man is also part owner of a topless bar and has a girlfriend who is a Russian prostitute.

The criminal Tony and the righteous Tony become grotesquely connected after a soccer coach in his daughter's high school impregnates one of her friends. The moralistic Tony goes ballistic. The criminal Tony considers enlisting his cronies to carry out a savage act of vigilante justice.

Along with Gandolfini and Marchand, Edie Falco (as the loyal but sharp-tongued Carmela),

Bracco, and Michael Imperioli, who plays Christopher Moltisanti, Tony's dumb, hot-headed nephew, who itches to be a "made" member of the Mafia, have the roles of their lifetimes in the series.

In many ways, *The Sopranos*, more than the wobbly, histrionic *Godfather, Part 3*, is the real sequel to Francis Ford Coppola's *Godfather* movies, which evoked the rise of Mafia in America as a parallel shadow image of corporate America. *The Sopranos* flagrantly borrows such dramatic techniques from *The Godfather* movies as crosscutting between scenes of extreme violence and domestic warmth, and interspersing the narrative with semi-hallucinatory flashbacks.

The thugs, especially Christopher, are so entranced with the mystique of *The Godfather* that they quote (and sometimes misquote) its dialogue. Christopher impatiently aspires to the imperial glamor of Marlon Brando and Al Pacino, and one episode found him working on an inept screenplay about mob life in the absurd assumption that a screenwriting and acting career are just around the corner.

But as much it owes to *The Godfather*, *The Sopranos* also refutes the towering solemnity of the Francis Ford Coppola films. Tony and his pals have none of the royal demeanor of *The Godfather*'s kingpins. Most are crude, bigoted, semi-literate boors who seem slightly out of place in the contemporary world. The criminal world in *The Sopranos* is strictly small potatoes, and it's fading. Tony, who's smarter than his colleagues, realizes that this seamy little society with its grim Old World code of loyalty, is becoming obsolescent, but there's not much he can do about it. *The Godfather*'s Corleones were made of sterner stuff. Even in their worst nightmares, they wouldn't dream of taking their problems to a shrink.

Some of *The Sopranos*' finest scenes take place in Dr. Melfi's office. Bracco's cool-headed psychiatrist drops all the right buzzwords, gently prodding her client toward insights into his childhood and his relationship with his parents, and dispensing anti-depressants and tranquilizers when needed. Her give-and-take with Tony may be the most realistic depiction of therapy ever depicted in a mainstream movie or television show.

Tony even develops a classic case of transference (drawn out in eerie, erotic dream sequences) in which he briefly imagines he's in love with the doctor. But *The Sopranos* ultimately dismystifies psychotherapy as much as it does the world of *The Godfather*. Psychotherapy proves useful for Tony (it supplies him with some clever managerial strategies), but it hasn't the slightest impact on his criminal character.

In forcing us to empathize with a thug whom we watch committing heinous acts, *The Sopranos* evokes a profound moral ambiguity. One of the series' most haunting moments finds Tony's teenage daughter Meadow crouched on the stairs furtively watching her parents remove guns and cash from a hiding place in preparation for an imminent search by federal agents. How does a nice middle-class teenager deal with the fact that her adored father is a thief and a killer? In the first season's most poignant moment, she bluntly inquires, "Dad, are you in the Mafia?" during a car trip to Maine where she and Tony are visiting colleges (and he slips off at one point to murder an FBI informant he happens to see at a gas station).

The Sopranos walks a fine line. As much as it banalizes its mobsters, it refuses to trivialize their viciousness. Tony's brutality is all the more disturbing because it erupts from within a social framework of apparent normalcy. That framework includes a devout young priest, who, like Dr. Melfi, skillfully sidesteps the deeper moral issues of Tony's life. The closest Tony comes to admitting evil is during a therapy session in which he offers the lame excuse that what he does is no worse than a businessman illegally dumping toxic waste.

But isn't that how we all get by in life without tearing ourselves to pieces? For aren't all values relative? In such a moral climate where everything is viewed on a sliding scale, it's easy for Tony to excuse himself, and say, adopting his best macho swagger, "You gotta do what you gotta do."

ADDICTED TO A MOB FAMILY POTION

BY
CARYN JAMES

Everyone in therapy talks about mom, but Tony Soprano has a unique family problem. "What do you think?" he asks, outraged at his psychiatrist's suggestion. "My mother tried to have me whacked 'cause I put her in a nursing home?" Well, maybe. In *The Sopranos*, HBO's brilliantly nuanced series about a suburban New Jersey mob boss in emotional crisis, the psychiatrist is helping Tony cope with this breakthrough: in the Sopranos' world you truly can't trust your own mother.

When the series began [in January 1999], Mama Livia Soprano was an irascible old woman, addled and comic enough to hit her best friend accidentally with a car. By the time Tony asks that question in the first season finale, she has come to resemble a maternal figure with roots in Greek tragedy and even Roman history. Her name should have been a clue from the start. An earlier Livia was the Emperor Claudius's ruthless, scheming grandmother (embodied by Sian Phillips in the miniseries *I, Claudius*). Both Livias are matriarchs who know how to play a bloody family power game.

Livia Soprano's darkening character is simply one strand in the complex web of *The Sopranos*, which has become more absorbing and richer at every turn. The series has pulled off an almost impossible feat: it is an ambitious artistic success, the best show of 1999 and many others; it has also become an addictive audience-pleaser, the rare show viewers actually talk and get excited about.

Nancy Marchand, who at first seemed unconvincing as the typical Italian mother, has turned Livia into a singular character. Tony was always more than the easy joke about a modern mobster on Prozac, stressed out by the demands of the job. James Gandolfini plays Tony with a deftness that masks the heft of a tragic hero, with flaws that might make him hateful and a visible soul that evokes sympathy.

Such depth helps explain why *The Sopranos* belongs among the classic miniseries. In its leisurely use of the form, it is strangely like *Brideshead Revisited, The Singing Detective,* and *I, Claudius* (whose historical figures have often been compared to a modern Mafia family).

Because the end of [HBO's original] 13-week series [commitment] was always in sight, it could develop the self-enclosed dramatic tension of a feature film: in the end, would his Uncle Junior take out a hit on Tony in a move to control the family business, or vice versa? Yet it also took the time to create ambiguous characters and the feel of a world through dozens of impeccable small touches.

With its flashy characters and human depths, *The Sopranos* suggests how thoroughly the Mafia wise guy has become ingrained in American culture, the stuff of both family tragedy and satire. Physically, Tony displays the trappings of a cliché. Overweight with a receding hairline, he wears a jogging suit, gold bracelet, and pinky ring. He is a killer. Yet as he frets about his children's education, about whether to put his mother in a nursing home, or about whether an old friend has worn a wire for the F.B.I. and has to be killed, his emotional pain is real. Tony is the mobster as a suburban family man (with bimbo girlfriends on the side) but also as a sensitive '90s guy who wasn't loved enough as a child. Emphatically middle-class, he is like one of your neighbors, but with a more dangerous job; that strategy allows viewers to sympathize and experience vicarious danger at once.

David Chase, its creator, is largely responsible

for *The Sopranos*, but the series' dual essence has been captured most succinctly in an unlikely place: a tag line created by an advertising agency. The ad shows Tony with his mob contacts on one side and his mother, wife and two children on the other; the line reads, "If one family doesn't kill him, the other one will." There is no better statement of the way the two sides of Tony's life converge to give the series its suspense and emotional power.

The earliest episodes only hinted at how rich and tangled its themes would become. The turning point came in Episode 5, when Tony took his daughter, Meadow, to tour New England colleges. Riding in the car, she asks him if he's in the Mafia; at first he denies such a thing exists, then admits that maybe some aspects of his business, ostensibly garbage hauling, are not entirely legal. It is a surprisingly touching conversation, a moment of painful honesty in which the father admits his imperfections and viewers sympathize with his paternal emotions.

Yet while driving Meadow around, he happens to spot a man who once ratted on the mob, then foolishly left the witness protection program. While his daughter is talking to a counselor at Colby College, Tony tracks down the man and garrotes him on camera. Without destroying sympathy for Tony, the series rubs viewers' faces in the fact that he is a murderer.

That on-camera violence, so crucial to the audience's complex, visceral response, is one reason *The Sopranos* could only appear on cable. On network television, his character would surely be sanitized, the violence toned down, the ambiguity cleared up and the entire series diminished. The brilliance of *The Sopranos* depends on the trick of letting us see Tony's worst qualities and getting us to identify with him anyway.

In a later episode, his psychiatrist, Jennifer Melfi (Lorraine Bracco), mentions her patient to her ex-husband, who warns: "Finally, you're going to get beyond psychology with its cheery moral relativism. Finally you're going to get to good and evil, and he's evil." But that voice, from an incidental character, sounds like a disclaimer. It is out of step with the experience of watching *The Sopranos*, which is gripping because it is so fraught with moral relativism.

Dr. Melfi remains the weakest link in *The Sopranos*, perhaps because she is not truly family. Occasional hints that she will be drawn into Tony's world (he once had a crooked cop tail her on a date) have gone nowhere, and she has remained the ultimate outsider. Viewers, who share Tony's experiences, are more a part of his family than she is.

In fact, feeling inside a Mafia family has become a cultural touchstone. There is some logic behind the coincidence that *The Sopranos* shares a premise with the 1999 hit film *Analyze This*, a slight comedy in which Robert De Niro hilariously plays a mobster who, like Tony, suffers panic attacks and ends up at the psychiatrist. Psychiatry is common today, and it is irresistibly funny to imagine a mob boss who is an emotional wreck.

More telling, together these works suggest how deeply Mafia movies have penetrated American culture. In *Analyze This*, Mr. De Niro sends up his own classic roles in films like *The Godfather, Part II* and *GoodFellas*. In *The Sopranos*, Tony's men model themselves on movie mobsters. One man has a car horn that blares out the first bars of *The Godfather* theme; another routinely impersonates Al Pacino as Michael Corleone. Tony's stupidly impulsive nephew, Christopher (Michael Imperioli), tries to write a screenplay about his mob experiences and longs for tabloid fame. Frustrated at his unimportance, Christopher complains that every movie mobster has his own story arc. "Where's my arc?" he says. "I got no identity."

Tony himself is smarter. When he is taken by a neighbor to play golf at a country club, he is bombarded with questions: "How real was *The Godfather*?" and "Did you ever meet John Gotti?" He may be a killer, but viewers feel for him at that moment; he is wounded at being condescended to and reduced to a cliche.

These '90s mobsters, after all, are a generation removed from the movies that inspired them. *The Sopranos* knowingly hits cultural nerves by responding to the present moment. Meadow reveals the truth about their father's business to her younger brother, Anthony, by showing him a Web site that features pictures of mob bosses. "There's Uncle Jackie!" says Anthony as he spots one of his father's best friends. (*The Sopranos* has its own place on HBO's Web site, which includes a section on the rock-inspired music that is so integral to its realistic feel.)

In the next-to-last episode [of the first season], Tony becomes so depressed he can't get out of bed. Even in this crisis, the series maintains its focus on the credible details of ordinary life. Tony's wife, Carmela, is perfectly played by Edie Falco with a toughened exterior that suggests how she has had to steel herself to her husband's profession. Carmela says, "If you want me I will be at Paramus Mall getting your son a suit for his first formal." One shrewdly drawn plot involves a situation that is absurdly common in real life but rarely discussed. Carmela has a flirtation with a priest, Father Phil, who comes to the house for ziti and movies before safely fleeing back to the church.

The final episode [of the first season] reaches a crescendo of action and intrigue, guilt and retribution. It sets up the story for the next season. And the cumulative weight of the previous weeks adds a delicious resonance to everything Tony says. When he tells a friend whose restaurant he has ordered set on fire, "I didn't burn down your restaurant, I swear on my mother," what exactly does he mean?

EVEN A MOBSTER NEEDS SOMEONE TO TALK TO

BY
CHARLES STRUM

The concept for the new hour-long HBO series *The Sopranos* sounds simple enough: an upwardly mobile Mafia capo from North Jersey slams head-on into a midlife crisis, enters therapy and starts taking Prozac.

Funny? Sometimes. Scary? Sure. Human? Very. But simple? No. It's about as simple as trying to dispose of a fresh corpse in the Meadowlands after dark when the lip of the construction Dumpster is just too high to reach.

"I was looking for the notion that life is so complex now that even a wiseguy needs help sorting it out," says David Chase, the creator, writer and co-executive producer of the series. "Plus, the mob as we know it has taken some pretty heavy hits from law enforcement. On a realistic level, who's to say that a man involved in this wouldn't be feeling tremendous pressure?"

That man is Tony Soprano (James Gandolfini), and the stress of heading two families, the one he lives with and the one he works with, is bared to his psychiatrist and the eavesdropping television audience. The audience sees Tony in all his many guises, including the inner Tony, a man not fully understood by his wife, his girlfriend, his passive-aggressive mother, or his two teen-age children.

But help comes from one of his own, an Italian-American therapist. She is Dr. Jennifer Melfi, a new kind of role for Lorraine Bracco, one of the movie screen's more famous mob wives. (Ms. Bracco portrayed Karen Hill, wife of the mobster Henry Hill in *GoodFellas*.) Having lived through Mafia home life, Ms. Bracco suddenly finds herself in designer suits and eyeglasses, asking questions like, "How does that make you feel?"

In preparation, she said, she thumbed through books with titles like *Going Sane*, *Sexual Feelings in Psychotherapy*, *The Intimate Hour* and *The Drama of the Gifted Child*.

Tony is a gifted child?

"Of course he's gifted," Ms. Bracco fairly shouted.

"It's heartbreaking," she said. "How could you

not like a man who is searching to do the right thing? It's *Father Knows Best* for the millennium. Tony comes to me with these mother issues, a powerful, grown man crying about not knowing what to do."

His wife and his daughter are at each other's throats, and his mother, Livia (Nancy Marchand in a startling departure from her famous WASP roles), dispenses guilt with the skill that comes only from generations of genetic honing.

How can any therapist possibly break through? Tony is a guy. A big Italian guy. He has big cars and a big white modern suburban house with a circular drive and a big in-ground pool, plenty of money (cash, usually), and more on the way.

Then comes the panic attack, and he ends up on the couch.

"Lately I get the feeling that I came in at the end," he tells Dr. Melfi, speaking of his work, his life, the really important challenges that confronted his father's generation. "The best is over."

"Are you depressed?" Dr. Melfi asks. Tony demurs, then fumes.

"Whatever happened to Gary Cooper, the strong silent type?" he says. "That was an American. He wasn't in touch with his feelings. He just did what he had to do. See, what they didn't know is that once they got Gary Cooper in touch with his feelings they couldn't get him to shut up. It's dysfunction this, dysfunction that."

As for Tony's ostensible career as a "waste management consultant," Dr. Melfi is cautious. As her patient starts to explain the stress of a recent business transaction—"We saw this guy, and there was this issue of an outstanding loan"—Dr. Melfi interrupts to point out that anything discussed in her office is private, but that if he were to reveal something about, say, a murder, she would be obliged to go to the authorities.

"I don't know what happened with this fellow," Dr. Melfi starts to say, but then Tony breaks in with a sincere smile.

"Nothing," he says, pausing. "We had coffee." At which point the camera leaves Tony's face and refocuses on an office park in Paramus, N.J., where the delinquent debtor, having spotted Tony, drops his tray of takeout coffee and tries unsuccessfully to escape Tony's fists and feet. All in a day's work, which frequently provides evidence of Tony's tough—even inventive—side. At one point, he assaults another wiseguy, using a staple gun to fasten the man's jacket to his chest.

For Dr. Melfi, the brutal Tony is not such a big issue.

"Look, I can only approach it in a way that is

best for him clinically, medically," Ms. Bracco said. "Getting into a discussion of stapling the guy's suit to him is not going to help me crack his psyche open to see the good and evil."

Ms. Bracco originally read not for this quiet, contemplative part, but for Carmela, Tony's wife, played by Edie Falco.

"Actors, we want roles that chew the scenery up," Ms. Bracco said. "But I was interested in a character no one has given me before. She's so controlled. She's a blank wall. This is almost like not speaking.

"She's not just a psychiatrist, she's from the neighborhood, you know? How many Italian-American educated women have you seen on screen?"

Ms. Bracco grew up in Bay Ridge, Brooklyn; her "big, powerful Italian father" worked at the Fulton Fish Market. As Dr. Melfi, she reins in the street-corner Brooklyn dialect that is her customary way of chatting.

Which leads to the question of Italians and stereotyping, and whether *The Sopranos* is likely to come in for some criticism.

Mr. Chase, whose family name was originally DeCesare, and the HBO-Brillstein Grey Entertainment production team see no problem. Neither do the cast members, almost all of whom are Italian-Americans from the New York-New Jersey area. Mr. Chase grew up in North Caldwell, N.J., in Essex County, where the Sopranos live, and insisted on filming at locations throughout northern New Jersey.

Mr. Gandolfini called the show an "equal opportunity drama."

"Certain things lend themselves to drama," he said. "It didn't bother me at all. I think people are ready for a certain lack of political correctness. We do things with some respect."

It also appears to be true to mob life in the '90s and the notion that art imitates life imitating art; that is, today's gangsters like to model themselves after their screen idols. The series is peppered with overused epigrams from Hollywood mob melodramas. In the scene in which Christopher (Michael Imperioli) and his partner (Vincent Pastore) try to dispose of a body in the Meadowlands, Christopher intones, "Louis Brasi sleeps with the fishes."

"Luca Brasi. Luca, Christopher," the partner corrects.

Celebrating a big cash haul at Newark International Airport, another crew member, Paulie (Tony Sirico), invokes Edward G. Robinson when he exults dramatically but pointlessly, "Is this the end of Little Rico?"

And crew members analyzing a recent rubout

ruminate on the significance of killing someone by shooting him in the eye. Citing primary source material, they discuss the death of the casino owner Moe Green in *The Godfather.*

"It's so funny because it's so real," said Chris Albrecht, president of HBO Original Programming. "These characters are all completely relatable. The only difference between Tony Soprano and me is that he's a mob boss."

Is Tony Soprano not so different from the Wall Street sharks who live down the block? Perhaps only in that he carries a .45 and they don't.

"I understand him," said Mr. Gandolfini, who grew up in Park Ridge, in North Jersey. "He can be brutal and compassionate. I think that people who have a lot of compassion also have a lot of anger. With some people the anger gets stuck."

Yet the compassionate side is often within reach.

In [the first season], Tony and his 17-year-old daughter, Meadow, drive to Maine to visit colleges. Cruising along in the family's light-gray Lincoln, a pensive Meadow suddenly turns to her father and asks, "Are you in the Mafia?"

"Am I in the what?" Tony says. "That's total crap—who told you that? That's a stereotype, and it's offensive. I'm in the waste management business. Everybody immediately assumes you're mobbed up. There is no Mafia."

But Tony's practiced lying is momentary, and he relents with one of the few people in the world he loves unconditionally.

"Look," he says, "some of my money comes from illegal gambling and whatnot." A pause. "How does that make you feel?"

"Sometimes," Meadow says wistfully, "I wish you were like other dads." But she has already inherited the Soprano coyness. She just needed to hear it from him.

Later, at dinner, the conversation continues, and in a single moment, with his daughter's face shining in the candlelight of a restaurant, Tony the son, Tony the father, and Tony the striver merge to confront the newly self-absorbed Tony.

"My father was in it, my uncle was in it," he says. "There was a time there when the Italian people didn't have a lot of options.

"Maybe," he adds, "being a rebel in my family would have been selling patio furniture on Route 22."

HBO WANTS TO MAKE SURE YOU NOTICE

BY
BILL CARTER

Spike Lee was there; so were Christopher Walken and Aiden Quinn and Stephen King and the present and former police commissioners of the city of New York. The party at Roseland on Wednesday night was the biggest ever given by HBO, no stranger to lavish premiere parties.

But then HBO has never before had anything quite as big as *The Sopranos* to promote.

The cable channel had planned on about 1,000 guests; about 1,800 showed up for the party and screening of two episodes in the new season. The Ziegfield theater could not contain the crowd, so HBO bused the latecomers to its headquarters on Avenue of the Americas. On the way they may have glimpsed one of the many *Sopranos* billboards dotting the city, or at least seen a city bus go by with the

cast glaring out in full menace just above the message, "Family: Redefined."

Had some taken the subway, there's a chance they could have ridden in one of the cars "fully branded"—as HBO's top marketing executive put it—with *Sopranos* advertising: nothing but black-and-white images of the cast.

It is all part of what Eric Kessler, the executive vice president for marketing at HBO, called a campaign "comparable to the biggest thing we've ever done." And why not, he added, "We're talking about the return of the best show on television."

The Sopranos won that label from virtually every critic last season. And for a show that is unarguably the most talked-about series ever on HBO, a channel that puts a premium on generating talk, the effort to reintroduce it to the public is extending just about everywhere HBO can reach. That includes HBO.com/Sopranos, of course, the most-used Web site ever associated with HBO, executives said. It features ersatz F.B.I. files on each character, gossip about who may be rubbed out and polls on the season's favorite lines of dialogue. (Last season's winner was uttered by Anthony, Jr. in Episode 1, about the absence of his grandmother's cherished ziti. Like many *Sopranos* lines, it can't be printed here.)

Then there are the CD of songs from *The Sopranos*, a music video, a traveling "waste management" truck (Tony's not-so-true calling), and a series of on-the-air promotions on multiple cable channels. There's even a promotion on a broadcast network, CBS, with the most prominent and expensive of those ads scheduled during the N.F.L. playoff games this weekend.

The promotional campaign is huge for HBO, both in significance and expenditure, though Mr. Kessler and other HBO executives declined to give an overall price. *Sopranos* images are so widespread, on display at bus stops as well as the entrance of Lincoln Tunnel, that some of the cast and crew are beginning to worry about a backlash. At the premiere party, James Gandolfini, who stars as Tony Soprano, said, sounding as if in character, "I'm sure people will be gunning for us this year."

Jeff Bewkes, HBO's chairman, said the pay cable channel was only trying to make up for "the big marketing disadvantage" it faced in comparison with the established broadcast networks. Only about 25 million subscribers receive HBO, about a quarter of the homes that are available to the broadcast networks.

"We are literally forced to buy buses," Mr. Bewkes said.

And trains. Mr. Kessler said HBO had also bought space on Metro North trains. That's just New York awareness, of course, he said. For more national exposure, HBO has turned to magazines like *The*

New Yorker, Vanity Fair, People and *Entertainment Weekly*, all of which will be running a four-page ad on *The Sopranos.*

Nothing is likely to be seen more widely than a commercial on an N.F.L. playoff game, but even there Mr. Bewkes said HBO was hamstrung. "CBS is the only network that will allow us to buy time," he said. And CBS forbids HBO to give the time and date of the *Sopranos* season premiere (Sunday at 9).

"Tony Soprano's Waste Management" truck will appear in parking lots at the N.F.L. playoff games and at the Super Bowl. Cardboard cutouts of the characters will be available for fans to pose with for pictures.

The channel also expects MTV or VH-1 to begin running a video featuring the show's theme song, "Woke Up This Morning," by the group A3.

This season's episodes include cameo appearances by people like Janeane Garofalo, Sandra Bernhard, Jon Favreau and Frank Sinatra, Jr., all playing themselves.

Many of them joined to other celebrities at the premiere at the Ziegfeld and the party at Roseland. It was one more indication of how far the show has come. Last year's premiere was in the basement of the Virgin Megastore on Broadway, and the party was at John's Pizzeria on West 44th Street.

—January 11, 2000

FROM THE HUMBLE MINI-SERIES COMES THE MAGNIFICENT MEGAMOVIE

A SEASON ONE REVIEW BY VINCENT CANBY

Movies and television have been feeding off each other for years, each trying to capture whatever part of the mass audience is the other's territory. In this age of political strategy dictated by public opinion poll, movies and television behave like a pair of rival party candidates for the same office: each side quietly adopts policies that differ from the other's only in degree, rarely in substance.

When innovative thinking is discouraged, choices dwindle in art as well as politics. Movies imitate television as television imitates movies that imitate television. While the screens in so-called home entertainment centers are getting bigger and bigger, movie theater audiences, with increasing frequency, carry on as if at home, talking, swilling their sodas and chomping junk food labeled lite.

And why not?

Today's audiences have been conditioned. A theater is simply a first-run outlet for material that will be seen again in the living room. Pop theatrical movies and television dramas are essentially the same: a dependence on close-ups, on shock effects and on pacing of narratives to bridge commercial interruptions, whether the interruptions exist now or are to be inserted later.

When there are exceptions, they usually come from independent and foreign filmmakers, seldom from television sources.

Thus, the effect is tonic when something turns up as singular as *The Sopranos*, HBO's 13-episode, nearly 13-hour melodramatic comedy, created by the seriously talented David Chase. It is also an event that prompts an examination of what our films and our television series have become and what their possibilities are, given the circumstances in which they are produced and the contexts in which they are seen.

The Sopranos did not emerge whole and complete like a sonnet from a single artist working in splendid isolation. Rather, it came out of the same rough-and-tumble process by which teams of collaborators have traditionally put together everything from soap operas, police and hospital dramas and sitcoms to shows as idiosyncratic as Roseanne's and Fraiser's.

It's not too much, I think, to compare *The Sopranos* to such seminal works as *Berlin Alexanderplatz* (1980), Rainer Werner Fassbinder's 15 ½-hour adaptation of Alfred Doblin's epic 1929 German novel, and *The Singing Detective* (1988), the tumultuous six-hour British production based on Dennis Potter's original script about the physical and moral redemption of an overly imaginative sinner with a skin condition. Both were created to be seen as television mini-series, which they were.

The Sopranos, shown as what was, in effect, a mini-series, was produced in the hope that it would become a continuing HBO series if successful, which it was. Thirteen new episodes have already been filmed, to be broadcast starting in January [2000].

Berlin Alexanderplatz, *The Singing Detective* and *The Sopranos* are something more than mini-series. Packed with characters and events of Dickensian dimension and color, their time and place observed with satiric exactitude, each has the kind of cohesive dramatic arc that defines a work complete unto itself. No matter what they are labeled or what they become, they are not open-ended series, or even mini-series.

They are megamovies.

That is, they are films on a scale imagined by the big-thinking, obsessive, fatally unrealistic Erich von

Stroheim when, in 1924, he shot *Greed*, virtually a page-by-page adaptation of Frank Norris's Zola-esque novel, *McTeague*. Stroheim intended it to be an exemplar of cinematic realism.

He also imagined audiences with cast-iron constitutions. His first cut ran nine and a half hours. He later reduced the running time to something less than five hours. Yet before *Greed* was sent out to theaters, the film had been taken away from him and others had removed more than three-quarters of the master's original material.

In 1950, after being persuaded to look at the mutilated final version in the archives of the French Cinematheque in Paris, Stroheim is reported to have said: "This was like an exhumation for me. In a tiny coffin I found a lot of dust, a terrible smell, a little backbone and shoulder bone."

Had television and the mini-series format been available 75 years ago, it is possible that Stroheim would have been spared his humiliation. *Greed* might have survived in something resembling the director's version. It could have been one of history's first megamovies.

Now we have mini-series, though few of these have the tight focus and consistency of tone associated with the megamovies I've mentioned. The English adaptation of Jane Austen's *Pride and Prejudice* qualifies. The *Brideshead Revisited* mini-series might qualify, even if, for me, anyway, it has the mournful expression and rouged cheeks of something embalmed. Unlike *Berlin Alexanderplatz, The Singing Detective* and *The Sopranos, Brideshead* never achieves its own identity. This may be because the novel, which it recreates with solemnity, itself seems a romantic and pious literary exercise compared with Waugh's comic masterpieces *Decline and Fall, Vile Bodies,* and *A Handful of Dust.*

The Sopranos, about the world of a New Jersey Mafia kingpin who seeks the help of a psychiatrist after suffering acute anxiety attacks, is no spinoff of *The Godfather* films or any kind of variation on the Robert De Niro-Billy Crystal comedy, *Analyze This.* It's a stunning original about a most particular slice of American life, a panoramic picture that is, by turns, wise, brutal, funny and hair-raising, and of significance to the society just beyond its immediate view.

Equally important is the way *The Sopranos* calls to mind the collaborative process that was accepted in Hollywood before every director considered himself an "auteur," to give the director the status of artist and largely to ignore the collaborators. In truth, the term auteur, as it was used by Francois Truffaut and his colleagues in the New Wave of French filmmakers and critics in the 1950s, was reserved for those directors of pronounced personal style and vision. In recent decades, though, it has become simply a fancy way to identify anyone who manages to receive a credit as a director.

The manner in which *The Sopranos* came together sounds initially less like Truffaut's now-classical auteurism than the old days at MGM or Warner Brothers or 20th Century Fox. This would cover the Hollywood studio system from the 1930s into the 1950s, when a production chief like Louis B. Mayer, Jack L. Warner, or Darryl F. Zanuck vetted every film on his lot, changed directors at will, recut films to his tastes, and secretly assigned writers to rewrite scripts not yet completed by the original writers.

No less than 11 directors receive credit for *The Sopranos* (two of whom each directed two segments), as well as eight writers (who sometimes wrote alone, sometimes in pairs or in threes) and two different directors of photography.

As the man who conceived the project and who, as the executive producer, kept its large team in harness, Mr. Chase is the show's undisputed auteur. He wrote and directed the first episode, took solo writing credit for another, and collaborated on scripts for two others.

Though *The Sopranos* received 16 Emmy nominations, the members of the Academy of Television Arts and Sciences, a traditional base for broadcast (as opposed to cable) television, finally gave the show only two awards. James Manos Jr. and Mr. Chase shared an award for the script of the fifth episode. Edie Falco was voted best actress in a drama for her performance as Carmela Soprano, the Mafia boss's wife, a loving, worried, common-sensical woman who aspires to respectability.

The production was budgeted to come in at $1.9 million to $2 million per episode, which would have made the total cost in the neighborhood of $26 million. That is small change by standards in Hollywood, where $26 million is not an outrageous budget for a comparatively plain, contemporary two-hour movie. By those same standards, *The Sopranos*, as a nearly 13-hour feature film, might have cost $169 million, without even trying to sink the *Titanic*.

In describing the production of *The Sopranos*, Mr. Chase makes it sound like the process by which a platoon of great comedy writers, ruled by Sid Caesar, put together the seminal Caesar shows of the 1950s. According to Mr. Chase, the writers of each *Sopranos* segment would meet to discuss ideas, sometimes augmented by suggestions from the other writers. Everybody chimed in. Each segment was shot fast—eight days—though they often went into overtime. There was a good deal of reshooting and a certain number of disagreements. That is, everything was perfectly normal.

Mr. Chase's background is in television, commercial and cable, where his credits as a producer, writer and director include *The Rockford Files*, *I'll Fly Away* and *Northern Exposure*. Nothing he had done before, though, was preparation for the achievement of *The Sopranos*. Here is the comic, frequently tortured journey toward self-awareness of Tony Soprano, affluent suburban family man, loyal son to a brutish mother, loyal Mafia member, extortionist and unhesitating executioner.

His immediate problem as he sees it: his business as a "waste disposal consultant" is "trending downward." More deep rooted are moral crises. Tony is a guy who is moved to scary (to him), inexplicable tears when he remembers a family of migrating ducks that had made an extended stopover in his expensive swimming pool, then suddenly abandoned the pool to continue the flight north.

The seamlessness of the direction, the writing, the photography (here is one show in which every close-up has a point and the camera never loses sight of physical context) is matched in the ensemble performances by the breathtaking cast.

Most notable: James Gandolfini (the heavy-lidded Tony, an assassin with sweet instincts he can't comprehend, a nascent beer belly and a short fuse), the splendid Ms. Falco, Lorraine Bracco (Tony's psychiatrist, whose treatment of her patient results in problems for both that Freud never dreamed of), Dominic Chianese (Tony's aging uncle and immediate mob superior, who is nearly undone by his longtime mistress), and Michael Imperioli (Tony's raging nephew, who aspires to be both a "made" man of the mob and a screenwriter). Dominating every scene she is in is Nancy Marchand as Tony's mother, a tough, emotionally stingy woman who wears a frown as her umbrella. It is she who instigates the kind of revenge on a son (he doesn't love her enough) to which only a mob widow and mother has access.

I saw *The Sopranos* not as it was initially broadcast at the rate of one segment per week, but at my own pace on cassettes supplied by HBO. Once I watched four together, another time three, but always at least two. This gives the critic an edge over the general public. Momentum builds. Small but important details that might otherwise be forgotten from one week to the next, or simply overlooked while one is attending to the plot, remain vivid.

Yet such privileged viewing also has the potential to create the sort of intimacy that makes it easier to spot lapses in continuity, contradictions within characters and a too-ready reliance on story formulas. *The Sopranos* not only survives such close inspection, but also benefits from it. A series like *Law and Order* does not. If cassettes are one way to establish that intimate contact, syndication is another.

How we respond to television fare depends on the manner in which we see it. Commercial-free premium cable channels, as good as they are, still lock one into someone else's scheduling. Cassettes are ideal, but there aren't that many mini-series or megamovies at the corner video shop.

Though the networks still dominate the television market, their audiences are dwindling. More and more people are apparently realizing that so-called free television demands too high a price: that we surrender an ever-increasing proportion of our attention to the contemplation of commercials. Since the rules were changed during the Reagan years, broadcasters can stuff any program with as many commercials as they can get away with. Only children's programs are regulated.

There are ways to avoid commercials, of course—riding the remote, going to the fridge—but in the long run commercials win: it's just too much trouble to run away.

In our society we celebrate advertising as an art form, which it may be. Advertising also helps to keep the economy going. Yet no child grows up today without being aware of the gulf between the real world and the world as seen in television commercials and in much of the entertainment they support. Isn't it possible the resulting skepticism eventually can evolve into something more pernicious: an unfocused, closeted cynicism that explodes in violence of no easily recognized motivation?

Such are the thoughts suggested by a show as fresh and provocative as *The Sopranos*, which has nothing to do with advertising but a lot to do with the temper of American life, especially with the hypocrisies that go unrecognized.

At one point, Tony tries to persuade Meadow, his teen-age daughter, that, although he has mob connections, her life is no different from those of the doctor's children who live next door. Her reply: "Did the Cusamano kids ever find $50,000 in Krugerrands and a .45 automatic while hunting for Easter eggs?"

There is a difference. Meadow knows it. So does Tony. *The Sopranos*, which plays as a dark comedy, possesses a tragic conscience.

—October 31, 1999

THE SOPRANOS: A SEASON ONE OVERVIEW

BY
RALPH BLUMENTHAL

His favorite uncle tried to have him whacked, his terrified shrink skipped town, his best friend may have betrayed him, and his malevolent mother, whom he was about to suffocate with a pillow, has just had a stroke. And you think *you* have problems?

With that and lots of other baggage, Tony Soprano and his gang of endearing mob misfits and dysfunctional kin embark on a second season of the runaway hit series *The Sopranos* on HBO. Last year's 13 episodes about an existentialist New Jersey Mafia boss in training to become a human being became the most lionized television phenomenon of 1999, winning legions of new customers for HBO and garnering 16 Emmy nominations, but in the end taking away only two awards. (Maybe the Emmy voters never heard what happens to people who rob the mob.)

Still, the family that preys together stays together, and so *The Sopranos*—with James Gandolfini as Tony, the lout with doubts and a human heart; Edie Falco as his sage and forgiving wife, Carmela; and Lorraine Bracco as Tony's ultra-professional yet enigmatically tempting psychiatrist, Dr. Melfi—are back with 13 new episodes that could be the prelude, its producers say, to a third season and perhaps more.

"The new episodes prove the show has room to grow," said Brad Grey, the executive producer who teamed up more than three years ago with David Chase, a writer, to create the series out of Mr. Chase's primordial issues with his own difficult mother.

Just don't ask them what's in store this season. They could tell you. But then they'd have to kill you.

HBO has given out some clues, however, and inevitably, with reporters invited to watch tapings at the Silvercup Studios in Long Island City, Queens, other tidbits have been leaking for weeks.

It is known, for example, that Tony Soprano visits Naples. His long-estranged older sister, Janice (played by Aida Turturro), driven away by their crafty beast of a mother, Livia (Nancy Marchand), returns home. After Jackie Aprile (Michael Rispoli), the acting boss of the Soprano family, died of cancer in Episode 4 last year, his menacing brother Richie (David Proval) now shows up, boding ill for Soprano family harmony. Dr. Melfi gets analyzed by *her* shrink, played by the director Peter Bogdanovich. Uncle Junior (Dominic Chianese), who put out the botched hit on his nephew Tony and then was arrested in an FBI sweep, gets out of jail. Into Tony's checkered love life comes an old flame, played by the stage actress Mary Louise Wilson.

In another innovation this season, Michael Imperioli, who plays Christopher, Tony's violently unstable nephew and a would-be screenwriter, makes the unusual transition to a writer of one of the episodes. "I always used to write in my basement," said Mr. Imperioli, who is no neophyte: he was co-writer of *Summer of Sam*, the Spike Lee movie about the paranoia set off by the serial killer David Berkowitz.

One other confidence can be revealed, as one of the season's directors, Tim Van Patten, imparted to this reporter: "People get whacked."

Just don't ask who. And don't ask what happened to Big Pussy Bompensero (Vincent Pastore), Tony's beloved sidekick and then suspected rat who disappeared mysteriously in Episode 11.

Last season's finale provided a powerful springboard into the new season. Here's how viewers left the Sopranos in April (and in subsequent reruns):

After conspiring with her pet brother-in-law, Uncle Junior, to have Tony, her own son, murdered out of pique that he might be complaining to his psychiatrist about her, Livia suffers a convenient memory loss. When Tony does complain to Dr. Melfi about his mother, and the shrink sympathizes with him, Tony leaps at her viciously: "That's my mother we're talking about!" They make up, but after the FBI rounds up Uncle Junior and 15 other members of the family (but not Tony), Dr. Melfi is spooked enough to take Tony's advice and flee town, leaving Tony shrinkless.

Feeling besieged on all sides and suffering existential angst ("What kind of person can I be when his own mother wants him dead?"), Tony rebuffs FBI efforts to turn him into an informant. He goes to the hospital determined to take care of his mother once and for all—he ominously snatches a pillow on the way to her room—just as she is wheeled out in the throes of an apparent seizure. But, under her oxygen mask, why is she smiling?

It all ends on a poignant note, with Tony, Carmela and their two untamed children, Meadow and Anthony, Jr. (Jamie Lynn Sigler and Robert Iler), finding refuge from a storm (metaphor alert!) in a friend's restaurant, where two of Tony's underlings, Paulie Walnuts and Silvio Dante (Tony Sirico and Steven Van Zandt), privately predict his imminent recrowning as family boss. Tony raises a glass to his brood: "Someday soon you'll have families of your own, and if you're lucky you'll remember the little moments like this that were good."

Whether the new episodes will meet the high expectations raised by the first 13 will have to be seen, but if they do—and Mr. Chase and many of the same writers and directors worked on the new season for Brillstein-Grey Entertainment—*The Sopranos* is likely to be a prime contender again at this summer's Emmy Awards. Last year Ms. Falco won for best actress and Mr. Chase for best writing of a drama series, but other series nominees, including Mr. Gandolfini, were ignored, to the consternation of many critics who saw the results as evidence of the networks' reluctance to accept cable television channels as full industry partners.

If the show's success is widely attributed to the superior writing and the inspired casting of a universe of miscreants with human foibles, the actors, directors and producers have no quarrel with that. In fact, a number of them said in recent interviews, the company has bonded to an extraordinary degree. "It feels at times like we've been together in a past life," said Ms. Falco of her on-screen marriage to Mr. Gandolfini. "Our jaws drop at how comfortable we are with each other."

Ms. Bracco, who came up with the idea of transporting the cast to the Emmys last year all together in a bus, said, "There's something so fabulous about loving all the cast and crew." Where it became artistically dicey, she said, was in the highly charged sexuality Tony brings to his sessions with Dr. Melfi, who, Ms. Bracco said, struggles to remain professionally aloof, to the point of wearing her hair shorter and her skirts longer.

"He's very attracted to me, I know," she said. "I have to be very careful. If I gave M Soprano an inkling of interest, he would eat me up and spit me out."

So where will it end? Is *The Sopranos* destined to continue season after season into the television record books? Mr. Chase won't rule it out, but he's cautious. "From my standpoint," he said, "there is a point at which a television series becomes a walking dead parody of itself. I hope we see it and shoot ourselves in the head first."

—January 9, 2000

DAVID CHASE: THE SON WHO CREATED A HIT— THE SOPRANOS

BY
ALEX WITCHEL

David Chase, the creator of the HBO phenomenon *The Sopranos*, picked me up at noon. We were driving to Elizabeth, N.J., for lunch at Manolo's, a restaurant he used as a location in the series—one that the mobster Tony Soprano torches.

"Do you really want to go to New Jersey?" Mr. Chase asked uneasily.

"Well, yes, I guess so," I said, a bit thrown. It had taken weeks of phone calls to arrange this meeting, since Mr. Chase is more than a little press-shy. "I thought you wanted to go to New Jersey."

"I didn't want to go," he insisted.

"You didn't?" I asked.

"No, I thought you did."

"Well, we don't have to," I said, trying desperately to think of an alternative.

He looked surprised. "Oh, I don't care if we go."

At that moment I realized there would be no need to speak to Nancy Marchand, who plays Livia Soprano, mob mother from hell. I had just seen the real thing.

Mr. Chase has created a cast of characters for his smash hit show who are completely idiosyncratic and unforgettable. But it is Livia—a mother so angry at her son for moving her to a nursing home that she helps put a hit out on him—who is a little more unforgettable than the rest. She is, of course, inspired in part by Mr. Chase's own mother, Norma, who died five years ago at the age of 84.

"She was, uh, a complete original," Mr. Chase said, seated at a corner table at Manolo's. He laughed uneasily, looking down at the tablecloth. "She had this incredible thing where she was very easily offended, yet there was never a person on earth who censored herself less. The way she acted was very sad. As she got older, she started insulting more and more people, taking umbrage at things they said and cutting herself off from the world. At a time when she was getting older and people die or get sick anyway, she was shrinking her circle by her own doing. It was very odd."

Mr. Chase said his parents had "married pretty late, in their early 30's." His father, Henry, was born in Providence, R.I., his mother in Newark, though both sets of parents came from Italy. Mr. Chase is an only child and neither of his parents was Roman Catholic: his father was Baptist; his mother, the 10th of 11 children, was reared by a "socialist atheist" father who loved opera and named some of his daughters after his favorites, including Norma and her sister Livia.

Mr. Chase was born in Mount Vernon, N.Y., but he won't say when. He worries about revealing his age in youth-obsessed Hollywood, though he offers "50-ish" as an estimate. He will also not give his daughter's name or where she will attend college. He says it was his paternal grandmother who changed the family name from DeCesare to Chase, but he won't say why. "It was a situation of l'amour fou" is as far as he'll go, worried that relatives will get angry if he divulges more.

His mother was a worrier, too, he said. "She worried about cancer, car accidents, criminals breaking into the house. And my father did get cancer. So did all her sisters."

What did Norma Chase make of her only child, a graduate of New York University who earned a master's in film from Stanford University and won Emmy Awards for his writing and directing of the hit series *I'll Fly Away* and *Northern Exposure*?

He grimaced toward the tablecloth and closed his eyes, something he did often. He seemed to keep hoping that when he finally opened them, I would have disappeared.

"I don't know," he said. "I was so far out of her world. My first directing job was an episode of *Alfred Hitchcock Presents*, and I called to tell her and she said, 'Really? Did they accept it?' " For as many times as he has obviously told this story, he still gasps with the disbelief of a hurt child.

" 'I don't cater to anybody,' she used to say. But there was a kind of self-awareness of what she was doing. Sometimes I would think: 'She's doing performance art. It's a character she's made up.' She was aware sometimes that she was being outrageous and provocative."

When Mr. Chase was 5, the family moved from Mount Vernon to Clifton, N.J., where Mr. Chase got A's in everything except deportment, in which he got F's. "I was out of my chair, talking a lot," he said. "I was always jiggling." Even now, sitting at the table, his hand drums its edge, then fools incessantly with a straw wrapper. When he was in seventh grade, the family moved to North Caldwell, N.J. His father owned a hardware store in Verona, and Mr. Chase worked there on Saturdays when he was growing up.

"I hated doing it, naturally," he said. He made another grimace. "My father had quit his job as an engineer in the early '50s and opened this Main

Street hardware store right when places like E. J. Korvette were just beginning. It never really took off."

His mother always worked, Mr. Chase said. For the most part, she spent her career with the telephone company, proofreading directories. He half smiled. "She had the ability to be in both places at the same time," he said. "She would say 'I hate it' and later say 'I didn't say I hate it; I don't know where you got that from.' " Which is very much like Livia Soprano, who Mr. Chase says wields "the tyranny of the weak."

"They orchestrate a lot of disturbance and require a lot of coddling and special attention just to get them to stop," he said. "All anyone wants to do is give them what they want."

No one is all bad, of course. What is his fondest memory of his mother? "I have lots of them," he said. "Once she got me some Ray Charles records for Christmas, which was not her kind of music at all. I knew she'd gotten them and where she had hidden them and one night I was drinking at my house with friends. I got them out and played them. I felt so warm and appreciative. And she didn't yell."

Mr. Chase says that his family was not involved in the Mafia, though he adds, "I was crazy about the Mafia since I was a kid." Watching *The Million Dollar Movie* helped. Even now, he can—and does—recite most of *Public Enemy* complete with a description of camera angles. "It blew my mind. It hooked me. I don't know why, but it did."

It seems completely out of character that Mr. Chase has lived in Los Angeles for the last 28 years. He has no tan, no real color in his face at all. He is balding and his hair is gray. And rather than preening about his new-found success, he doubts his good fortune, scared somehow that it will be taken away. He is sure he is about to contract "a horrible illness."

Is it time to go back into therapy? He shrugged. The character of Dr. Jennifer Melfi (Lorraine Bracco) reflects Mr. Chase's own experience with a female therapist, though he says he saw "three or four men before that and they all did me some good." One heavy-breathing speculation about *The Sopranos* is that Tony (James Gandolfini), who is treated by Dr. Melfi, will have an affair with her. Though Mr. Chase is careful not to divulge too much of what will happen [in the second] season, his response to this is definite.

"Ludicrous," he fumed. "The hiding and shame is not what the show's about. And the therapy would be ruined."

The Sopranos is shot on location in New Jersey, and at the Silvercup Studios in Astoria, Queens. It is staff written, meaning Mr. Chase and three or four other writers work together on "beating out stories."

Mr. Chase directs some episodes; he also casts, edits and scores them.

"The second year was never planned out," he said. When HBO rescued the series, it had been rejected by the networks and Mr. Chase couldn't see past the first season. "What concerns me most now is the noise from the outside world," he said. "Can we keep this up? Last year my feeling was only 'we have nothing to lose.' "

As for how many more seasons fans can hope for, Mr. Chase is noncommittal. "Given the life that Tony's in, it can't go on forever," he said. "Something has to happen."

For now, though, he says he loves writing for this cast. "As a writer I usually start off in a defended position. For example, I put three dots at the end of a sentence so it will trail off and then the actor reading it ends the sentence. I used to think actors were only there to ruin everything. They terrified me. I had a sense with actors that they have all the fun, that they're less responsible than the rest of us. It made me jealous. I came to it late, but I see now that they're the best part of it."

As for directing, Mr. Chase said: "It terrifies me. That first time-directed, the *Alfred Hitchcock* show, I was so scared that the night before I had thoughts of going to the Greyhound station and leaving L.A. It felt like the time I was 11 and sprained my ankle on a camping trip and went to visit my grandmother in Mount Vernon. And my aunt had just had a baby and for some reason I wanted to carry him. My ankle gave out and I dropped the baby. I ran out of the house screaming. Directing felt like that. I felt lame with the whole thing."

"I've always been anxious, fearful, competitive, envious, and angry," he went on matter-of-factly, talking about his drive to succeed. "When I'm on the set, though, I don't freak out. I say to myself, 'You know what, this looks like life, but it's not. Whatever happens here isn't going to kill you.' " The grimace finally slid into a smile. "That's about the best I can do."

YOU CAN'T TELL THE PLAYERS WIDDOUT A SCORECARD

BY

J. MADISON DAVIS

James Gandolfini

plays

ANTHONY SOPRANO

Life's not getting any easier for Tony Soprano, but he might just be adjusting to being the head of the family. Maybe the therapy's slowly working. He acts with more authority and shows less obvious doubt. Uncle June seems to have accepted Tony's leadership. Richie's visiting his brother Jackie—permanently—and the FBI surveillance has gotten nowhere.

That's not to say Tony hasn't got plenty to worry about. He's still not a Happy Wanderer, and that family of ducks that stopped at his swimming pool still haunts him. Something's strange about New York *capo* Johnny "Sack" Sacramoni moving out to New Jersey—are they cutting in? Ralphie Cifaretto is a major pain, and that business with the garbage contracts threatens to blow the whole operation sky high. Anthony, Jr. seems to be a chip off the old block—in all the wrong ways. Meadow's getting educated in a way that's making her forget who her real family is. Tony couldn't keep his promise to the dying Jackie Aprile to protect Jackie, Jr., a kind of adopted son for Tony. And, of course, he's still got issues with Livia, dead as she may be. Why couldn't he have a mother like Jimmy Cagney's in *The Roaring Twenties?* And Johnny Boy, his father, who introduced him to the meatier aspects of gangsterdom, still tortures his subconscious.

Tony seems to spend his time trying to make peace among the family, dealing with Janet antagonizing the Russians, with Ralphie's loony acts, with Christopher and Paulie screwing up a simple collection. And what's with that woman selling Lexuses? Doesn't she understand that he has sex just to have sex? Carmela's a rock, but it doesn't do too good to push her; she's getting a bit moody sometimes.

Tony's tired of trying to solve everyone else's problems, but he can't escape his sense of obligation to do so and seems to be moving closer to accepting the role. He can't control things like he thinks he should, but maybe he's becoming smarter and more confident about the ways of power. Before Jackie died, Tony's solution to preventing a hit in Artie Bucco's restaurant was to burn the restaurant down, rather than assert himself against his uncle. Now, he'd be more likely to issue an order, though who knows if it will be obeyed in the way he wants. Furio Giunta from Italy has been totally loyal to him, and he's used him effectively. He sniffed out Big Pussy's betrayal, but can't be quite sure that damaging information hasn't gotten to the FBI. Yet, he still can't quite feel like Vito Corleone and can't grasp why. He wants it to be 1954 in his house, but it isn't. A guy like him shouldn't be talking to a psychiatrist, but what's his choice? It seems to help.

JAMES GANDOLFINI continues to rack up the awards and nominations and awards for his portrayal of Tony Soprano, including Emmys (winning in 2000 and 2001), a Golden Globe nomination, a Screen Actors Guild nomination, an American Film Institute award, and a Television Critics Association award. Although he had been in many movies before *The Sopranos*, all the attention has moved him into much better roles on the big screen. A versatile actor, he was astonished to be chosen for the lead role in *The Sopranos*. "Look at this face," Gandolfini once said to other cast members. "They took *this face*. What were they *thinking*?"

After he graduated from Rutgers University, he spent some years as a bouncer and nightclub manager. In the early 1980s a friend took him to an acting class. Everyone seemed to recognize his talent but him, and he has never had a better opportunity to show the extent of it than on *The Sopranos*. Tony, says Gandolfini, "tries to do the right thing in his mind," but Tony's mind is nothing like the usual pseudo-Don's or series hero's. That's what makes his performance so realistic and powerful. The hardest thing about playing Tony Soprano, says Gandolfini, is learning the lines.

Gandolfini made his Broadway debut in 1992, and has appeared in a number of plays on and off-Broadway, including revivals of *On the Waterfront* and *A Streetcar Named Desire*; early in his career, he toured Scandinavia in the latter. His more notable movies include *Fallen, A Civil Action, Twelve Angry Men* (on HBO), *8 MM* (with Nicholas Cage), *Night Falls on Manhattan, She's So Lovely, A Stranger Among Us* (his film debut), *The Juror, Get Shorty, Crimson Tide, The Mighty* (with Sharon Stone), and *True Romance*. Look for him with Kathrine Narducci (who also plays Charmaine Bucco) in the short film *A Whole New Day*, which occasionally airs on Cinemax; he plays a drunk who misplaces his wife and apartment. In last year's film *The Mexican*, with Brad Pitt and Julia Roberts, Gandolfini played a gay hit man, and was generally considered to have stolen the show from his more famous co-stars. He also appeared in the Ethan and Joel Coen production of *The Man Who Wasn't There*, with Frances

McDormand, Michael Badalucco, and Billy Bob Thornton, as well as *The Last Castle* with Robert Redford, Delroy Lindo, and Robin Wright. Recently, he's expressed a strong interest in playing bus driver Ralph Kramden—the role immortalized by comic actor Jackie Gleason—in a widescreen version of *The Honeymooners*.

Afraid of losing Gandolfini permanently to the big screen, HBO signed him to a generous contract after the first season, but the short season for the show, which keeps fans hungry for more, also allows him ample time to work on other projects. Initially, he was attracted to *The Sopranos* by the "bizarre" good writing in the scripts, in which sudden turns from humor to violence keep viewers off-guard. Gandolfini appreciates the realism of the series—it is filmed in New Jersey, for one thing, where he was born in Westwood in 1961.

Gandolfini hit the gossip pages this year when he filed for divorce against his wife of only three years, Marcy Wudarski. They seemed a devoted couple before that ("very Italian," said Gandolfini), and have a three-year-old son, Michael. The reason for the sudden divorce? As is typical of Gandolfini, of his private life he ain't talking.

Edie Falco

plays

CARMELA SOPRANO

What's up with Carmela? In a man you might call it a mid-life crisis. In earlier seasons, she was a rock, occasionally shaken, but steady; now, she's opening up. She's confronting the feelings she suppressed about Tony and the family business. In a startling moment, the psychiatrist she visits on Dr. Melfi's advice tells her she will never feel right about herself until she gets rid of Tony. And—who knows?—she's capable of it. Carmela is, in some ways, tougher than Tony. While he can murder a man with his bare hands, she has put up with Tony's constant philandering and his depressions, not to mention her children's crises, and still had the energy to deal with Tony's mother.

At Livia's memorial service, however, Carmela cut loose and slapped down all the evasions and hypocrisy. Over many years of marriage, she developed the ability to avoid thinking about the machine guns and wads of cash in their heat ducts. But she was never really passive, however. There's a volcano of passion in Carmela that's always threatening to erupt. She copes by buying furniture, secretly investing in the stock market, and trying to widen the social circles in which she and her husband move. She had Father Phil for spiritual solace, too— at least until she recognized that the priest used food and DVDs to dance a little too close to the carnal flame of the lonely women he counsels. And then, what came over her when she was redecorating the powder room? That clinch with Vic Musto (played by Joe Penny) was throwing matches at a gasoline tanker truck. She's not afraid to confront Tony, wants to know everything that's going on, and doesn't hide her feelings, but that much explosive passion would scare anyone. Now that the kids are older, maybe it isn't worth it as much to look the other way.

An accomplished stage actress, EDIE FALCO says she researched the role of Carmela by being born into a boisterous (though non-Mafia) Italian family. Her father is jazz drummer Frank Falco. She graduated from the acting program at the State University of New York at Purchase, whose alumni are nicknamed "The Purchase Mafia," and worked some as a clown at birthday parties. For *The Sopranos*, she

The late Nancy Marchand

played

LIVIA SOPRANO

Producer and writer David Chase named Tony's mother, Livia, after a maternal aunt and gave her many of the characteristics of his own mother. However, she also shared the name of Augustus Caesar's ruthless, scheming wife in the celebrated BBC production of *I, Claudius,* which seems more than coincidental. In the first few episodes she seemed to be little more than a declining old woman—afraid to leave her house, afraid of being sent to a nursing home, constantly harping on the way it used to be. She soon, however, showed the manipulative and calculating character that led to Dr. Melfi's opinion that she had a borderline personality disorder. Tony was more direct in his diagnosis: He said his sisters fled her at the first opportunity, and that she wore his father "down to a nub." She was grinding on Tony as well, and seems to have passed her scheming genes on to her daughter Janice. Nothing Tony or Carmela or anyone could do was adequate, whether it was buying the right pastry or cooking pork.

Livia was too crafty to be direct, except with rude and meaningless complaints. Once settled in the retirement home, she received regular visits from Junior and dropped snippets of information that nudged him to various actions that he thought came from his own muddled thinking; in short, she played him like a fiddle. Only Tony seemed to see through her facade of being addlepated, and remembered the way she crushed his father's plan of making a new start in Reno. She once threatened to blind Tony with a fork and to suffocate her children. Nonetheless, these memories never relieved Tony's guilt at dealing with her. Carmela saw her for the monster she was, but treated her with respect for Tony's sake. Once, when Carmela mentioned Junior's visits, Livia protested too much, as if she felt something for Junior she shouldn't have. Livia was a bitter onion, layer upon layer of veiled possibilities. Was she willfully consenting to her son's murder, planting the idea in Junior's mind? Or was it senility? Was she pretending to have memory lapses? Or were they merely convenient? Did she fake her stroke? Or was it a coincidence?

Even after her death, Livia's poison still infects

all members of her family. She never saved Janice's schoolwork, and the silly memorial service at Tony's home erupts in recriminations.

NANCY MARCHAND, who brought Livia Soprano vividly to life, died on June 18, 2000, saddening the cast and millions of fans who appreciated her great talents. She had been ill with emphysema before beginning *The Sopranos*, and the writers had tentatively planned on Livia dying at the end of the first season. Marchand's portrayal, however, was so remarkable that they carried Livia into the next season, though her importance in the plot diminished. Michael Imperioli, interviewed by Dennis Miller on HBO, described how Marchand was a constant inspiration to the cast. Breathing with difficulty, she relied on bottled oxygen, but would set it aside when the cameras started rolling to become Livia Soprano. After her death, Marchand appeared briefly in the third season, thanks to the magic of computer generated imagery, much as actor Oliver Reed appeared in scenes of *Gladiator* after his death.

Born on June 19, 1928 in Buffalo, New York, Marchand's mother tried to cure the girl's shyness by enrolling her in acting classes. She attended Carnegie Tech and became quite successful in theater, winning two Obies and being nominated for a Tony. Meanwhile, Marchand appeared in numerous television programs going back to the *Philco Television Playhouse*, on which she played opposite Rod Steiger in Paddy Chayefsky's *Marty* in May 1953. She also appeared on the series *Naked City, Beacon Hill, The Adams Chronicles, Cheers, Night Court*, and many others. Although she is primarily remembered for her work in television, she acted in many films, including T*ell Me That You Love Me, Junie Moon, The Hospital, Regarding Henry, Jefferson in Paris*, and *Sabrina*. She is perhaps best remembered for her role in the series *Lou Grant* as Mrs. Margaret Pynchon, a part drastically different from Livia Soprano. This role as the aristocratic owner of the *Los Angeles Tribune* (suggesting Katherine Graham of the *Washington Post*) earned her four Emmys from 1978 to 1982. Altogether, she was nominated for the award seven times, including the two she received for playing Livia.

Jamie Lynn Sigler

plays

MEADOW SOPRANO

Meadow Soprano, Tony's daughter, is off to college and has lost all her innocence, Tony says. When we first met her she was in that horrible transitional stage when you never know whether you're going to be judged as a "young lady" or as a kid. Adults let you get a peek at their lives, then slam the door in your face. She was an honors student at Verbum Dei high school, playing volleyball and soccer. She wanted to go to Berkeley, as far away from New Jersey as possible, but her parents suggested Colby, Bowdoin, or some place closer, and Tony personally took her on a tour of such campuses. Like all teenagers, she pushed her worldliness to assert her independence and adulthood, making out with a Dominican boy, and trying to talk about sex (and being silenced by Tony).

However, Meadow is not as sophisticated as she

thinks. She knows her father is Mafia, yet isn't quite sure what it means and how to react to it. When Tony shows up with Eric Scatino's SUV as a gift for Meadow, it doesn't take her long to find out Eric's father lost it gambling in Tony's Executive Game. Can she live with that? In her first year at Columbia University, she hooks up with Noah Tannenbaum and gets serious. But he's half Jewish and half African-American, and Tony is not exactly liberated to the mixing of the races. There are some ugly confrontations, but Noah dumps her, because his father doesn't approve of Tony's background in "waste management."

And what's this about a Soprano singing? JAMIE LYNN SIGLER released her debut album in 2002, *Here to Heaven*, which features three of her own songs. She was seen belting out "I'm So Pretty" from *West Side Story* on a Bravo special celebrating Broadway, played the lead in the touring company of the musical *Cinderella*, and sang in a Levi's commercial. This is more than just indulging a wannabe pop star's fantasies. When Jamie Lynn Sigler was nominated for the Young Star Award for "Best Performance in a TV Drama Series," she was already a veteran performer. She enrolled in dance school at age three, and singing and acting lessons at seven. She had appeared in a number of plays in the New York area when she was signed to her first professional role at age twelve in the musical of *It's a Wonderful Life*. She took a national tour with the play, which ran for five months. She later appeared as the lead in productions of *The Diary of Anne Frank* and *The Wiz*, got her dream role in Les Miserables, and acted in the film *Brooklyn State of Mind* and the television horror series *Campfire Stories*. She maintained an A-average all through high school and took college level courses from Syracuse University in her senior year. She majors in psychology at New York University and hopes to have a career as a theater therapist. Her mother was Cuban and she grew up listening to Latin-style music, which is why four of the songs on her new album are sung in Spanish. She made the gossip columns this year by going public with her struggle against anorexia, and increased pulse rates in the world with a daring photo spread in the male magazine *Maxim*.

Robert Iler

plays

ANTHONY SOPRANO. JR.

A.J. is getting older, and Tony's worried that the acorn's not falling far enough from the tree. Anthony's having panic attacks. He drops like a rock on the football field when he's made defensive captain and flops to the rug when he tries on his military school uniform. Military school? Well, there was this thing about the vandalism at the Verbum Dei school. He got off the hook for that because of the school needing him for a football game and, probably, his parents' donations. But then there was the stealing of a test. That turned into an expulsion, and Tony wants to save A.J. enough to send him to military school.

When we first met Anthony Soprano, Jr. in the first season, he was just a Nintendo-playing couch potato with the typical irreverence for everything and distaste for his older sister. He downloaded porn, got into occasional fights, and was suspected of having Attention Deficit Disorder by the school counselor because he fidgeted in class—in other words, he was an ordinary thirteen-year-old. By Season 3, he's progressed to a Sony Playstation, but he's still confronting what it means to be part of a mob family. He has had a flirtation with nihilism after reading Camus, which, because it coincided with his Confirmation, utterly exasperated his parents. He did well on the swim team, but Tony, who had resolved to spend more quality time with him, showed up late. We may see a boy in the pains of growing up, trying to find out who he is, but Tony is afraid the boy is turning out like his father.

ROBERT ILER did a lot of growing up this year when he was charged with felony second-degree robbery and unlawful possession of marijuana. He, allegedly, with three friends, robbed a couple of sightseers of $40 in July 2001. He has steadfastly denied it, and as of February 2002 was refusing a plea bargain that would have required him to admit to the crime. Most of *The Sopranos* cast back him up and say he's not the kind of kid who would do such a thing.

Iler's acting career began when he was discovered at age six by a talent agent as he walked down a street in Manhattan. He has appeared in many commercials, including ones for AT&T and IBM. He has also appeared on *Saturday Night Live*, as well as in the film *The Tic Code*, with Gregory Hines, in which Iler plays a bully. His latest feature film appearance is as "Charlie" in *Tadpole* with Sigourney Weaver. He attends public school in Manhattan and was nominated for the award of "Best Supporting Young Actor in a Television Series" at the Twenty-first Annual Young Artists Awards.

Dominic Chianese

plays

UNCLE JUNIOR

Corrado Enrico "Junior" Soprano faced cancer in Season 3 and again proved himself to be a survivor—not many gangsters live long enough to get cancer. He's smart enough to run back up the stairs to avoid Janice's memorial service for Livia, and smart enough not to get drawn into Richie's schemes, but not smart enough to take over. As Tony's uncle, the older brother of "Johnny Boy" Soprano, he played catch with Tony when he was a kid and has racked up two convictions in the "business." Like Tony, he doesn't know what the world is coming to. The younger generation doesn't have values, and the old codes seem to be falling apart. He commiserated with Livia about the crumbling of his world, and they together idealized the past. He used to think Tony wasn't capable of running the family—imagine a *real* man seeing a

shrink!—but now he seems to think Tony is learning.

Anyway, he's got too much on his mind: He's
wearing a monitor on his ankle and can't leave his
house without permission, and the close call with
the cancer has him taking stock. Earlier, however,
Junior's fantasy of the way things ought to be
blinded him to the obvious. It was too easy for Tony
to set him up as head of the family and a lightning
rod for federal investigators. Trying to show his
strength, Junior taxed Hesh Rabkin (though Johnny
Boy never did), refused to move the hit planned for
Artie Bucco's restaurant (though it would destroy his
business), watched Mikey Palmice kill Christopher
Moltisano's friend Brendan, and set up Tony for a hit.
Yet, when Tony survived, Junior defiantly refused to
violate the *omerta* by feeding Tony to the cops. It
would also be weakness to be known for satisfying
his woman orally, and when the word got out, he did
a Cagney on her with (appropriately enough) a pie,
dumped her, and fired her. Tony's making fun of
him for going down was the last straw in making
him decide to put out a contract on Tony.

In the second season, confined by house arrest,
Junior enjoyed the company of a solicitous widow,
Catherine Romano, and was tempted by Richie
Aprile's designs on Tony. But Junior is a sager judge
of character, awing his bodyguard. He warned

Richie against Janice, who he sensed was behind Richie's ambitions—perhaps because Livia manipulated him in the same way—and then recognized that Richie was incapable of carrying out his own schemes. Junior seems to have decided that being alive is good enough, for the moment. Or maybe he's playing the fox. . . .

Junior is played by DOMINIC CHIANESE, who began his career in 1952 touring in Gilbert and Sullivan's *The Mikado* and *Patience*. He still sometimes works as a cabaret singer. He has been very active on the stage and in television, appearing in episodes of *Kojak, East Side, West Side, Dark Shadows*, and *Law & Order*, among others. He's done his share of mob films, with *The Godfather, Part II, The Lost Capone*, and *Gotti*. He's also seen in *Dog Day Afternoon, All the President's Men, Fort Apache: The Bronx, Night Falls on Manhattan, Cradle Will Rock*, and the popular remake of *The Thomas Crown Affair* with Pierce Brosnan. He was rewarded for his fine performance as Junior with an Emmy nomination for the second season.

Lorraine Bracco

plays

DR. JENNIFER MELFI

It's official: The American Psychoanalytic Association has a severe case of transference for Dr. Jennifer Melfi, declaring *The Sopranos* the most accurate representation of psychoanalysis to have ever appeared on screen. It doesn't hurt that Dr. Melfi is beautiful and never sexier than when she is wearing her most professional coolness. And then there are the anxieties of being a psychiatrist. There are a lot of feelings boiling around inside her. Should she be treating this thug Tony Soprano or not? She turns to her own psychoanalyst and mentor, Dr. Elliott Kupferberg, played by Peter Bogdanovich, but he can't really help. She understands Tony's problems, at least from a theoretical viewpoint, but his passion and brutality is far from her world. A graduate of Tufts University Medical School, she has a highly successful practice, but Tony fascinates and terrifies her.

Every ethnic group has its own dark side, and Italian-Americans live always in the shadow of the Mafia, disgusted with its legacy, yet attracted to it as well. When Dr. Cusamano's wife mocks the tacky Murano sculptures in Carmela's house, Melfi, with ambiguity in her voice, says she likes Murano. Her ex-husband belongs to an anti-defamation league and decries the Italian stereotyping in the media, but her son, a college student, points out to his father that mobster Joe Columbo founded the organization. Melfi is careful to avoid knowing anything specific about Tony's business, but is curious enough to stand awkwardly on a toilet at Dr. Cusamano's house to sneak a peak at Tony's house and imagine God-knows-what when she hears grunts. Even with the danger from both Tony and the mob, even when her internal conflicts are driving her to fortify herself with vodka before meeting with Tony, and even when Elliott asks her why she doesn't just drop Tony as a patient, she compulsively continues to treat him. Does she really think she can handle an enraged Tony with a pair of scissors? Is she feeling an erotic fascination with the low, just as Tony is fascinated with her sexy, upper-class refinement?

Season 3 really tested her feelings about Tony. Raped in the staircase of her parking garage and betrayed by the legal system, she has only to say the word and Tony will rip the rapist's throat out. Yet, she cannot do it. Whatever her fascination is with the dark side, she does not embrace it—at least for the moment.

LORRAINE BRACCO was an interesting choice for the role of Dr. Melfi, both because of her beauty and because of her playing the wife of mobster Henry Hill so notably in *GoodFellas*. She assumed she was being offered another mob wife role for *The Sopranos*, but life takes strange turns, however. Bracco was once voted the "ugliest girl in the sixth grade," according to one report, yet she became a fashion superstar after moving to France in 1974, and worked as a DJ on Radio Luxembourg. She has a daughter by Harvey Keitel, but is currently married to Edward James Olmos. She can be seen in *Hackers, Getting Gotti, Even Cowgirls Get the Blues, Medicine Man, Radio Flye*r, and *Sea of Love*, among others. Her latest films are *Custody of the Heart, Tangled, Riding in Cars with Boys* (with Drew Barrymore), and the televison movie *Sex in Our Century*. She has been nominated for an Emmy for both of the first two seasons of *The Sopranos*.

David Proval

played

THE LATE
RICHIE APRILE

How could two brothers turn out so different? When the wise Jackie Aprile ran the family, disputes were few and the garbage business was stable and profitable. But when Jackie's distinctly unwise brother Richie was released after a decade in jail, he was nothing but trouble. The business had changed, but Richie didn't want to hear about it. He figured he was due, and he wasn't satisfied with his cut.

What's more, he wasn't very subtle. When Beansie Gaeta owed him some money, Richie smashed his legs with a car. Tony wanted respect— but who is Tony, anyway? Richie moved around the Soprano family like a low-rent Richard Gloucester planning to hack his way to the throne. He even revived his old relationship with Tony's sister. Was it a way to get closer to the throne? Or was it a way to satisfy his need for weird sex? Actor David

Proval thinks Richie had real feelings for Janice and even Tony. Richie was hurt when Tony gave away a leather jacket that was a souvenir from a whacking. But when it comes to business, what's love? Fuhgeddaboutit!

Richie was evil, but not smart enough to get anywhere in the end. He misread Tony as weak, and Junior didn't get to be an aging Mafiosi by tumbling to schemes like Richie's. But his worst misjudgment was in thinking Janice was weak, too. The daughter of Johnny Boy and Livia Soprano wouldn't be slapped. She fed Richie a lead antipasto, and he ended up in someone's sausage.

DAVID PROVAL played Richie with evil oozing from his pores—so much so that the performance has been described as the most realistic portrayal of a gangster ever on television. Proval read for the part of Tony Soprano before James Gandolfini was selected. He grew up in tough Brooklyn neighborhoods and remembers the dead-eyed Richies who roamed the streets. He studied acting with Uta Hagen and William Hickey, and appeared in *Mean Streets*, *The Shawshank Redemption*, *Innocent Blood*, *Four Rooms*, *The Star Chamber*, *The Siege*, and several other films. He won a best actor award at the Toronto film festival for playing the retarded title character in the movie Nunzio. On television, he had a recurring role on *Picket Fences* as Frank the Potato Man. His most ironic role, however, was that of a rabbi opposed to the death penalty on *The West Wing*, just after Richie disappeared into the meat grinder. Apparently, they cast him without being aware of his role in the show that they would later battle for the Y2K Emmys.

Aida Turturro

plays

JANICE SOPRANO

If you had a sister like Janice, you might need psychotherapy as well. In the first season, Tony's sister Janice Soprano was described by Tony as a "fucking wanna be dot-head" who has taken the name "Vishnamatha or somethin'," but she remained off screen. Janice had run as far away from Livia as she could, as soon as possible. Drifting along the West Coast from Los Angeles to Seattle, she lived in a commune and adopted the name Parvati.

Because of Livia's stroke, however, she returned to New Jersey in the second season to give Tony even more family headaches. He doesn't trust her any more than he trusts his scheming mother and knows, just knows, that she's up to something. What is Janice up to when she gets Livia out of the retirement home and back into her old house? It can't be only daughterly devotion or sentiment—

she must be trying to find out about what Livia knows, particularly about hidden money. And then what's with the revived relationship with Richie Aprile? Is Janice using Richie to get what she wants, or is Richie using Janice? Or are they really in love? Or is it some combination? They certainly have a relationship that Krafft-Ebbing would have salivated over. Richie puts a loaded gun against her head during sex. But Richie makes the mistake of thinking Janice is just another woman to slap around. He demands dinner, and she serves lead.

Janice is soon headed back to the West Coast, but not for long. Soon she's back when Livia dies, stealing a prosthetic limb in order to get her mom's vinyl collection and causing Tony major *agità*. And who can forget that incredible memorial service Janice insisted upon? Let's all share something about mom, who never said a good word to anyone, who never kept my schoolwork, or encouraged me in the slightest way!

AIDA TURTURRO played James Gandolfini's wife in the 1992 revival of *A Streetcar Named Desire* starring Jessica Lange and Alec Baldwin. Gandolfini persuaded her to try out for the role of Janice. She is one of the busiest actors in the business, working on stage, screen, and television. She has appeared in dozens of films, including *Bringing Out the Dead,*

Mickey Blue Eyes, Fallen (in which Gandolfini also acted), *Sleepers, Manhattan Murder Mystery, Tales of Erotica, What About Bob?,* and *Play It to the Bone.* On television, she has appeared on *Law & Order,* and *Sesame Street,* and did a stint as "Fran" on *As the World Turns.* John Turturro, her cousin, directed her in the film *Illuminata.* Nicholas Turturro is another cousin, and Olinda Turturro is her sister. Aida's father was an abstract painter, and she grew up in a converted synagogue on the Lower East Side. The only job she admits to having had outside of acting is that of a home organizer. She says that the role of Janice has lifted her out of endless offers to play prostitutes, secretaries, and psychics. She was nominated for an Emmy for her work in Season 2. Known as one of the hardest-working actresses in show business, her latest film appearances were in *Crocodile Dundee in Los Angeles* and *Sidewalks of New York.*

Jerry Adler

plays

HESH RABKIN

Herman "Hesh" Rabkin has always been one of the inner circle of the Soprano family, and was always trusted by Johnny Boy as a *consigliere*. A Jew (do we hear the whisper of Meyer Lansky here?), Hesh can never be a made man, but that doesn't decrease his stature; gangsters weren't all Italians, after all. As the psychiatrist observes to Dr. Melfi in one episode, Louis Lepke and his boys were "some tough Jews." Hesh, however, worked with his brain more than muscle. He's a negotiator, not a fighter, but that doesn't mean he's weak. He was the front man for F-Note Records (Johnny was the silent partner), which exploited black artists and looted their royalties. Now he provides credit for those who can't get loans at Chase Manhattan, and finds peace in contemplating the horses on his farm.

*　*　*

JERRY ADLER plays Hesh, and has worked with producer/writer David Chase before on the quirky television hit Northern Exposure. He appeared in a number of other television series, including Mad About You, Quantum Leap, Law & Order, Hudson Street and Raising Dad. In movies, he is familiar as the neighbor Larry Lipton (Woody Allen) suspects of killing his wife in *Manhattan Murder Mystery*. He also had the role of Maurice Tempelsman in the television miniseries Jacqueline Bouvier Kennedy Onassis. He played a Jewish mob grandfather in Six Ways to Sunday and most recently appeared as a limo driver in Mixed Signals.

Michael Imperioli

plays

CHRISTOPHER MOLTISANO

Christopher Moltisano is a soldier of the MTV generation. His literature is the motion picture, and his nightmare is a life without a plot curve. He wants success quick and he wants it easy, constantly grousing about not being a "made" man yet, despite whacking a Czech gangster and finishing off Mikey Palmice. It's a material world for Chris, and he doesn't understand why he should be living in a cheap apartment, never mind his $60,000 Lexus. He also much too eager to take a toot now and again, which doesn't help him develop any patience. When Tony takes a trip to Italy, Christopher spends his entire time in a hotel room doing drugs.

To find a quicker way to the top, he gets himself screenplay books and sets out to write a mob picture on a stolen laptop, which doesn't seem to come with a spell checker. Chris manages to get involved with an independent film that features Janeane Garofalo and Sandra Bernhard. He also has an affair with his cousin's fiancée Amy, a woman in the film business who betrays some of his mob confidences to her boss, director Jon Favreau. They are just using him, he realizes, and when pressed by Tony to make up his mind—movies or the mob—he shows more loyalty than one would expect.

He decides to stay out of a heist his friend Brendan has planned against Tony's orders, but when it goes awry, he tries to get Brendan off the hook. He's devoted to his girlfriend Adrianna, a waitress with aspirations to be a music manager. He pays for the studio and arranges for her to make a contract with a record company, even though he comes to realize that the group stinks. The failures of his fantasies always keep his anger simmering, however. Why *not* make racial insults in an African-American burger joint? Why *not* shoot a pastry shop clerk in the foot?

The major crisis of the second season for Christopher involved his being shot by two stupid burglars as a gift for Richie Aprile. On the operating table, Christopher spends a moment clinically dead. His visit or dream of either Hell or Purgatory provokes not just a spiritual crisis for him, but also for Paulie Walnuts. In Season 3, Christopher finally becomes "made," but discovers it's an awful lot like work. Paulie demands his tribute payments for setting Christopher up and gets very angry when he's shorted. Paulie and Christopher also prove how inadequate they are in the Pine Barrens when they get lost trying to get rid of a stiff.

At Livia Soprano's memorial service, Christopher delivers a ridiculously rambling monologue on life and death that was perfected by several hits on a bong and a noseful of coke. Will the drugs get to him? Will Tony catch on, or face up to the obvious—and then what happens to Christopher?

MICHAEL IMPERIOLI plays the role of Christopher and has appeared in nearly forty movies since 1988, when he was only twenty-two. He is one of the most active young people in film in many of its aspects. He was recently a producer and writer for the Spike Lee film *Summer of Sam* and in September 2000 premiered *On the Run*, directed by Bruno de Almeida and co-starring John Ventimiglia (Artie Bucco on *The Sopranos*). Unlike Christopher, we can assume Imperioli knows how to spell, since he wrote the episode "*From Where to Eternity*," in which Christopher dies on the operating table and is revived. Among the more notable movies he has appeared in are *Trees Lounge, I Shot Andy Warhol, Dead Presidents, Malcolm X*, and *Lean on Me*. In *GoodFellas*, he plays "Spider," who is shot in the foot by Joe Pesci, and which is alluded to in Moltisano's shooting of the bakery clerk. His latest roles were as Rosencrantz in *Hamlet* (with Campbell Scott) and in *Love in the Time of Money*, but who knows where this multitalented player will show up next as writer, producer, or director? Imperioli owns a bar in the Chelsea area of Manhattan called Ciel Rouge.

Vincent Pastore

played

THE LATE BIG PUSSY BOMPENSIERO

Big Pussy" Bompensiero was one of Tony's inner circle, a reliable soldier, or so he seemed in the first episodes. He disappeared in episode 11 of the first season, much to Tony's distress. Alcoholic detective Vin Makasian (played by John Heard) said that Pussy was wearing a wire for the Feds, and Tony was ninety percent certain it was true. Pussy was a good man and they went way back, but with three kids in college and the business slacking off, Pussy might have cut a deal. Didn't his back pain and the Percodans indicate he was under great stress? Only at the last moment did Tony discover who was really wearing the wire, and that Vin owed Pussy thousands in gambling debts, but Pussy had meanwhile mysteriously vanished. Witness protection? Sleeping with the fishes?

Just as mysteriously as he left, Pussy returned

in the second season, and the plot thickened again. We discovered Pussy was, indeed, an informant for the FBI. He'd been nailed on a heroin deal and faced thirty years in jail. He even got into his role so seriously, he began to try to out-FBI the FBI. Simultaneously, he was plagued with guilt, breaking into tears at Anthony, Jr.'s Confirmation. It took a roaring case of food poisoning for Tony to piece together that Pussy was a traitor, something he refused to see. Paulie said Pussy was like a brother, but Silvio, Tony, and Paulie nonetheless consigned him to the fishes. Paulie admits in the Season 3 that he would kill him again if he had the chance.

VINCENT (VINNY) PASTORE, who played Pussy, owned a club in New Rochelle, New York, frequented by Matt and Kevin Dillon, who persuaded him to try acting. He had studied acting a bit in college, but had no idea how to get into the business until an agent guided him. He was already in his forties, but he got a break, appearing in *True Love*, which won the Sundance Film Festival, and then got noticed for his lengthier role in *Jerky Boys* with Alan Arkin. He's become a more and more familiar face through the 1990s, especially in gangster films such as *GoodFellas, Gotti, Who Do I Gotta Kill?, Witness to the Mob*, and *The Last Don*. In *Night Falls on Manhattan*, he worked with both James Gandolfini and Dominic Chianese, and he appeared in The *Hurricane* with Denzel Washington. He has also frequently worked in television, particularly on *Law & Order* and *Bull*. His latest movies include *Riding in Cars with Boys* (with Drew Barrymore and Lorraine Bracco), and *Last Laugh*, which was made for television.

"Little" Steven Van Zandt

plays

SILVIO DANTE

Silvio Dante runs the Bada-Bing! Club and is another member of Tony's inner circle. He appears to be Tony's most trusted colleague, ready to arrange a whacking without a question and participating in the killing of Big Pussy with a little regret, but no hesitation. With his hair (is that a rug or what?) a particularly unnatural color, Silvio looks a bit like *Saturday Night Live* comedian Kevin Nealon doing a skit. He is so obviously a mobster, his comments about raising kids in the information age or his arguments with the ref at his daughter's oh-so-suburban soccer game seem particularly other-worldly.

STEVEN VAN ZANDT, a guitarist with Bruce Springsteen's E Street Band, was considered for the role of Tony Soprano, even though he had never acted before. Producer David Chase saw Van Zandt on a music awards show and decided he'd be a natural. When asked to play another part, he wasn't sure he wanted to take a role away from an actor who had paid his dues, so Silvio was written in. Van Zandt says that playing in the E Street Band is the "greatest f**king job in the world," but he has looked into other art forms for much of his career. He presented a film in progress called *Men Without Women* at the Cannes film festival. He also wrote a musical of *The Hunchback of Notre Dame* which has never been produced because Disney considered bringing their film version to Broadway. Van Zandt says his version would have "kicked ass" compared to theirs. Van Zandt frequently tours and is one of those musicians who varies his sound quite a bit, something he says has harmed his career because he doesn't have a signature style.

"Little Steven" is also a strong supporter of animal rights, something we doubt Silvio is enthusiastic about. Notice the inside joke in the show that Silvio is said to have owned rock clubs in Asbury Park. Van Zandt once wrote that there are solo guys and band guys, and that he is the latter, which can be awkward for a guy going solo. Luckily for viewers, there is no awkwardness in how well he plays Silvio in the Soprano band.

TONY SIRICO

plays

PETER PAULIE WALNUTS GUALTIERI

The third member of Tony Soprano's inner circle is Paulie Walnuts, who got his name either from the hardness of his head or his mistake in hijacking a truckload of walnuts instead of televisions. He is a tattooed, old-fashioned thug with a few "issues" of his own—something about women, it seems. He even consulted a therapist, though he can't get his head around Tony's going to a *woman* psychiatrist.

Paulie is not without his deeper side. He is offended by the "rape of Italian culture." Why should non-Italians be getting rich on espresso and cappuccino? When Christopher is shot, Paulie has a spiritual crisis trying to understand Christopher's visions and even visits a psychic who spooks him pretty bad. He looks at Purgatory as just another form of jail term, the kind of thing he can do standing on his head. Paulie's a movie buff, quick with a quip, but deadly as a cobra. Business is business, and when Christopher doesn't fully keep up the tribute Paulie's supposed to be receiving, he shows his tough side. Late in Season 3, he's beginning to voice some dissatisfaction to Johnny Sack of the New York mob with the way Tony is running things. Could he be drifting? We'll find out next season.

His best episode this season was "Pine Barrens." In an early episode we saw how he hates poison ivy! Paulie and nature just don't mix. So when Paulie and Christopher go to the Pine Barrens to dispose of a body, they're in big trouble. That particular episode won a Writers Guild of America award for authors Terence Winter and Tim Van Patten, who once played "Salami" on *The White Shadow* television series. That particular episode won a Writers Guild of America award, as well as an Edgar Allan Poe award from the Mystery Writers of America for authors Terence Winter and Tim Van Patten. Van Patten once played "Salami" on *The White Shadow* television series.

Paulie is played with an interesting mixture of humor and utter cruelty by TONY SIRICO—and he knows whereof he speaks. Sirico is probably the only member of the cast who has the "penal experience" (as Tony calls it). He grew up poor in Bensonhurst and wanted to be like the gangsters he saw on the streets.

Among his crimes was the armed robbery of night-clubs. The result was a rap sheet with 28 arrests and two stretches in the big house, including time in Sing Sing. It was in prison that he saw a traveling ex-con theater group, and he says he had the revelation that he could stand up and bullshit people as well as they could. After his release in the early 1970s, he joined the Actors Studio. He got his first job in the film *Crazy Joe* in 1974.

Sometimes listed in the credits as "Anthony Sirico" or "G. Anthony Sirico," he's been in many gangster movies, including *Godfather II, Miller's Crossing, GoodFellas,* and *Mickey Blue Eyes,* but he's also been a regular in Woody Allen films, appearing in *Deconstructing Harry, Celebrity, Everyone Says I Love You, Mighty Aphrodite,* and *Bullets Over Broadway.* His latest roles are in *Turn of Faith* with Charles Durning and Ray "Boom Boom" Mancini, and *The Last Request* with Danny Aiello; in the latter, he plays a priest. Divorced, he lives in Bensonhurst with his mother and claims to make the world's greatest meatballs. He regularly gets advice on how to play Paulie from the wiseguys in the hood. One of the legends around Sirico is that he insists on a verbal agreement that he won't have to play a "rat." The *omertà*, you know.

Joe
Pantoliano

plays

RALPH CIFARETTO

The trouble with working with criminals is that many of them aren't very nice. Ralphie, in fact, is quite un-nice, and looks like he's headed for a reckoning with Tony. Ralph Cifaretto was a soldier under *capo* Richie Aprile until Richie disappeared into the sausage grinder at Satriale's, so in many senses in Season 3 Ralphie is a stand-in for Aprile, causing Tony major *agità*. Ralph has moved in with Rosalie Aprile, Jackie Aprile's widow, and takes on a stepfather role with Jackie Aprile, Jr., taking him on collections when Tony had promised Jackie Sr. to keep the boy out of the life. Ralph wants to be promoted to *capo*, but Tony puts Gigi Cestone in charge.

Ralph is unpredictable, and capable of unthinking violence. Obsessed with *Gladiator*, he re-enacts a scene, swings a chain at the Bada-Bing! Club, and puts out XXX's eye. In a later episode, one of the girls gets pregnant by him and it becomes clear he isn't going to do anything to support the child. He beats her to death, then tells Tony that she slipped and hit her head. Tony flies off the handle and pummels Ralph, something a made guy is not supposed to do without authorization to another made guy. He considers killing him, but when Gigi Cestone dies, Tony takes Silvio's advice and tries to heal the relationship. He goes ahead and makes Ralph *capo*, and when Jackie, Jr. robs a card game in Ralph's territory, Ralph simply has the boy capped. He's as sociopathic as Richie, but, so far, less of a plotter. He's already gone too far, too often, and looks like in any episode he'll finally get Tony's undivided wrath.

JOE PANTOLIANO says that he, like Tony Sirico, was saved from a life of crime by acting. Growing up in Hoboken, New Jersey, Pantoliano was raised on welfare in a public housing project. His father drove a hearse and had ties with the mob. His mother made book. The man separated from his wife when Joe was twelve, and the boy was well on his way to becoming a drug dealer or thief. At seventeen, he had only a third-grade reading level, but the need to study the scripts forced him to improve. He could now play shady characters rather than be one. He waited tables in Manhattan, studying acting under Herbert Bergoff and John Levine, and earned stage roles. In 1976, he moved to Los Angeles and began a number of appearances in situation comedies. He's a familiar face now for motion picture fans, with notable appearances in the movies *Risky Business, Empire of the Sun, Midnight Run, The Fugitive, The Matrix,* and *Memento.* He's also appeared on television in *NYPD Blue, Amazing Stories, The Fanelli Boys, EZ Streets,* and others, as well as several miniseries. He used his sinister presence to play attorney Roy Cohn in one miniseries, and assumed the Frank Sinatra role of *"Maggio"* in a re-make of *From Here to Eternity.* For his next project, Pantoliano enters the world of superhero action films with *Daredevil*—based on the popular Marvel Comics series—in which he stars opposite Ben Affleck, *The Scorpion King's* Michael Clarke Duncan, and Jennifer Garner, star of ABC-TV's hit series *Alias.* The film is slated for a January 2003 release.

Drea de Matteo

plays

ADRIANA LA CERVA

Adriana La Cerva is Christopher Moltisano's girlfriend, a waitress with the ambition to be the manager of a rock band. For all her toughness, however, she's a bit too innocent for a business like music. The band she wants to manage is led by a childhood friend whose talent is not entirely lacking, but who won't ever have a hit. Adriana won't accept that Moltisano may be right that the rap producer who may release the record is more interested in her bada bing than her band. In the second season, the role of Adriana was enlarged into one of the regular characters and we discovered that Richie Aprile was her uncle. It seems that all eyes are on Adriana in the third season, as her and Carmela's female tennis instructor, Jackie Jr., and Artie Bucco all take notice of her formidable physical assets. None of this attention is reciprocated. Carmela:

could she be a little miffed she's not the center of the tennis instructor's attention? When Adrianna resigns from her job at Vesuvio, Artie has dinner with her and later leaves Charmaine, but he confesses his feelings to Tony, not Adriana. Even Paulie joins in the hormonal storms she inspires by sniffing her panties—though he's mostly doing it to tweak Christopher for not living up to his obligations as a "made" man. Adriana has said she doesn't want to end up as a mob wife, but Christopher is moving up the ladder and could haul her up with him. He brings her stolen Jimmy Choo shoes. He and Furio are silent partners in Crazy Horse, the nightclub she now owns thanks to the former owner's bad football bets. Chris looks like the best prospect on her horizon, no question. Otherwise, why would she put up with that rambling meditation on life and death at Livia Soprano's wake? She'd better watch her own loose lips, however. Her new best friend is an FBI agent and Adriana might just say the thing that will put Christopher in the slammer.

DREA DE MATTEO, who plays Adriana, grew up in Whitestone, Queens, New York, and says that she got the job because of her blatant Queens accent, an accent she desperately worked to lose before her acting career. The daughter of a playwright and a furniture manufacturer, she originally intended to become a director, but got noticed for her acting ability while studying at the prestigious Tisch School of the Arts at New York University. When she auditioned for the part of an Italian bimbo on *The Sopranos*, producer David Chase didn't think she was very Italian. With her real name Andrea Donna de Matteo, she's not Italian enough? Later the accent burst out. She was soon promoted to Christopher's girlfriend for a couple of episodes and then kept being written into new episodes. Her movie appearances include *Meet Prince Charming, Swordfish, Deuces Wild*, and the still-in-production *Prey for Rock and Roll* with Joan Jett and Gina Gershon. Drea has been called a tough, chain-smoking rock and roller. She has an AC/DC tattoo on her belly and has her clothes made custom, by the same designer who creates clothes for Joan Jett and Steven Tyler.

Jason Cerbone

played

THE LATE JACKIE APRILE, JR.

Ah, the excitement of the criminal life, always on the edge, always exciting! Is it any wonder that young men are attracted to it? Get a little older and it doesn't seem so glamorous. Unfortunately, many of those young men never survive their youth. Jackie Aprile's dying wish was that his son would escape the criminal life and become a doctor. Tony promised to make that wish come true, but Jackie Jr. had other ideas. If dad was a gangster, if your uncle was a gangster, what's so wrong with that? Beats studying. Besides, Jackie Jr. knew the experts, and they gave him the education he really wanted.

Soon enough, he was the driver for Christopher's robbery of a concert. He went on collections with stepfather Ralphie. He got himself a piece and went to rob Gene Pontecorvo's poker game. But Christopher and Furio were there, and Furio got shot. Christopher went to Tony and demanded Jackie, Jr.'s head for shooting a "made" man, but Meadow was now dating Jackie, Jr., and it has looked like a match made in heaven after Meadow broke up with Noah Tannenbaum. Tony left the decision to Ralphie, despite his relationship with Jackie's mother. Did Tony imply what must be done? Or was he hoping Ralph would back off? Whatever his motivations, Jackie Jr. was later found dead in a tenement area in Boonton.

A native of Yonkers, New York, JASON CERBONE started his career in acting very early, appearing in a *Sesame Street* advertisement when he was two. Later he appeared in videos for Bon Jovi and Suzanne Vega. He suspended his acting career while earning a degree in biology from Concordia College in Bronxville, New York, though he says his interest in that kind of biology has now faded; like Jackie, Jr., he isn't headed for medical school. He has appeared in episodes of the television series *Third Watch* and in the feature films *Paper Soldiers, Collision Course*, and *Spike of Bensonhurst*. Jason says he enjoyed playing Jackie, Jr., simply because the boy put on a different face for whomever he was trying to manipulate—Tony, Meadow, Carmela, Christopher. During the season, there were rumors that Jason and Jamie Lynn Sigler were an item, though he denies it. Now, he says he is recognized on the streets, though people often say Jackie, Jr. on *The Sopranos* is taller and more handsome. Jason was named one of *People* magazine's "Top 50 Bachelors" in July 2001.

Annabella Sciorra

plays

GLORIA TRILLO

Men and cars, sure. Plenty of romance there. But men and their car salesperson? Gloria Trillo, however, is hotter than a Mercedes and exactly the psychological steam table that Tony can't resist. Do men always seek the same kind of woman? Are they always looking for mama no matter how destructive and twisted she was? Gloria doesn't seem anything like mama when Tony meets her, but he does meet her in Dr. Melfi's office, and maybe rushes her out for a liaison on The Stugatz without asking himself why she's seeing the doctor in the first place. We later find out she's got a problem with relationships. Her last one ended with her attempting suicide, but, she's nuts about Tony. They have sex in the reptile house at the zoo. How Freudian is that? It isn't long before all this heat starts her boiling over. She explodes when she hears about Tony's old girlfriend. When she gets over this she wants to make nice with a home-cooked meal, but ends up throwing the beef at Tony. Given all of Tony's memories of his father and Satriale's, this is a fine touch, but Tony nonetheless admits to Dr. Melfi that the relationship makes him happy. He underestimates Gloria's craziness, however. Soon she is taking Carmela on a test drive, quizzing her about the family. She calls the house and Tony tries to break it off. She calls the Bada-Bing, hysterically crying, and Tony nearly strangles her as she begs him to kill her. Finally, Dr. Melfi's point about the women Tony seeks gets home. Tony sends one of his soldiers to convince her their affair is over. She looks plenty terrified when the conversation is over, but who knows? Will she be back? Will memories of the snake house at the zoo be too much for Tony to resist? It is *amour fou* after all.

ANNABELLA SCIORRA was born Annabella Gloria Philomena Sciorra in Wethersfield, Connecticut, but grew up on the Upper East side of Manhattan. As a little girl, she used to sneak out of bed to watch television late at night and imagine being part of the show. Her compulsion to act, she has said, grew out of a need to escape her everyday existence. While most people are afraid that they'll be humiliated while performing, Annabella was afraid she was boring or ridiculous in real life. She becomes completely absorbed in the characters she plays, saying that the character cannot be separated from the actor. After high school, she went straight into acting, forming a theater company, and first attracting national notice in *True Love*. Usually in supporting roles, she has appeared in a number of commercially successful films, proving she has a good nose for good parts, avoiding less complex characters such as are in the many weak comedies released each year. She has appeared with Tim Robbins in *Cadillac Man*, with Richard Gere in *Internal Affairs*, as the romantic partner of Wesley Snipes in Spike Lee's *Jungle Fever*, and with Robin Williams in *What Dreams May Come*. She can also be seen in *The Hand That Rocks the Cradle, Cop Land,* and *Romeo is Bleeding*, among many others. She was an associate producer and appeared with Christopher Walken, Isabella Rossellini, Chris Penn, and Benicio del Toro in *The Funeral*. Her more recent work includes the Italian film *Domenica*, the television film Jenifer, and *American Crime*, which is in production.

A CABLE
SHOW NETWORKS
TRULY WATCH

BY
BILL CARTER

The Sopranos is such a white-hot favorite in the television industry that network executives are trying to figure out how they can copy the breakthrough style of the HBO series and perhaps make up for the mistake several of them made in passing up the show in the first place.

Interest in the cable show has reached such a fever pitch that two networks have even approached its production company to inquire about the possibility of running episodes of *The Sopranos* after they have appeared on HBO.

That seems unlikely, given the show's cable-standard content, which includes nudity, violence and enough florid street language to curl a network censor's toes. But Brad Grey, the executive in charge of Brillstein-Grey Entertainment, which owns *The*

Sopranos, has said, "The networks are calling now to ask if they can air the shows we've done already."

He would not identify the two networks that made the offer, but he said, "It never reached a serious stage because I just said no." He said he doubted the show could have been edited in a way that wouldn't compromise it creatively.

Besides, it is not as if the broadcast networks didn't have a shot at *The Sopranos* the first time around. The show was developed by the drama department of the Fox network in 1996, but it never went anywhere. Mr. Grey said the pilot script written by the show's creator, David Chase, "just came back with a no; we didn't even get any notes from them." Mr. Grey said he then "talked to CBS" about the show, but those conversations led nowhere. And, as usually happens with scripts in Hollywood, word of *The Sopranos* drifted around. One executive who heard about it was David Nevins, the senior vice president of prime-time series at NBC, who said: "I had a shot at it after Fox passed. I thought it was very good. But I couldn't get anyone else interested."

Now the networks are more than interested; they're fascinated.

As Carolyn Ginsburg-Carlson, the senior vice president of comedy for ABC put it, "I love the show; it's one of only three or four shows I make it a point to watch every week."

The Sopranos is already a hit by cable standards, scoring ratings higher than any cable channel series in the previous three years. In its Sunday night showing, the show is reaching about 3.7 million viewers, and in its four weekly showings it reaches more than 10 million viewers.

For the people who make television shows for a living, *The Sopranos* is more than an HBO hit; it is a groundbreaker, a show whose influence is likely to be felt throughout the industry in the coming years.

Warren Littlefield, the longtime NBC program chief who was scouting for talent to build his new production company [at the time the series first aired], said the show had prompted the industry to rethink what constitutes "family drama" on television.

"If you look at what network television has done with the family drama, it just made them all dull," Mr. Littlefield said. "We all had blinders on as to how you can present a family on television."

So are networks busy developing shows that will try to embrace the more outrageously creative approach of *The Sopranos*? Not yet, because most of their development was finished before the show went on in January 1999.

Counting itself lucky in terms of timing, CBS does have a Mafia-based drama in development. But its antecedent was the movie *Donnie Brasco*, not *The*

Sopranos. And even broadcast executives disagree on whether the networks could duplicate *The Sopranos* style.

How different is the HBO show from what the networks saw in 1996? Danielle Claman, the Fox drama executive who developed the show (and admits to experiencing a "personal loss" over failing to win support for it at the network) said: "It's 90 percent the same. The show's story is the same, but obviously it is spicier now that it's on HBO."

Mr. Nevins said the original script that he read would have been evaluated by the network standards department. He added: "I don't believe we couldn't do the show on NBC. Content-wise, you could take a little bit out and get it through."

Peter Roth, a former president of Fox Entertainment who is now running the Warner Brothers television studio, said, "I think *The Sopranos* is makable for a network. It could play on ABC on Sunday night after *The Practice*."

That is not how Chris Albrecht, HBO's president of original programming, sees it. "The networks would never have put the show on," he said, adding that what Fox developed as the original script is not the show that so impresses Hollywood now. He noted that HBO was willing to take a risk and allow Mr. Chase to direct the pilot himself.

Then there was the crucial decision to allow him to shoot the series on location in New Jersey.

The most important decision HBO made, Mr. Albrecht said—and that point was seconded by every other executive interviewed for this article—was selecting James Gandolfini to play the lead role of Tony Soprano, the gang leader who is so harassed by business and family problems (many of which overlap) that he goes into therapy.

Even one senior NBC executive, speaking on condition of anonymity, said: "If we had done the show, that guy would have never gotten out of the casting room. He is overweight and balding. Somebody would have said: 'He's no TV star. Get somebody sexy.' And we would have messed the whole thing up."

Ms. Claman said Fox had planned to use Anthony LaPaglia as Tony. Even HBO hesitated on Mr. Gandolfini, Mr. Albrecht said, but only because there were two other outstanding auditions for the role, by Steve Van Zandt (best known for his guitar work with Bruce Springsteen), who now plays a Soprano soldier named Silvio, and Michael Rispoli, who played Jackie, the gang leader who died of cancer midway through the first season.

Even if a network had taken the risk on Mr. Gandolfini, Mr. Albrecht said, other decisions would have rendered the show a pale imitation of what is on the air now.

"They would have tried to do New Jersey in L.A.," he said. "And they would have included commercials. You put in commercials and you change the dynamic."

Then there is the money. "They would try to make this for $1.6 million an episode," Mr. Albrecht said. "We're spending $300,000 to $400,000 more."

Mr. Littlefield is one executive from the network side who agreed that *The Sopranos* needed all the freedom that HBO provides. "You can't just take that content and language out," he said. "The content is part of that overall gestalt; it's part of what surprises you. Those surprises are one reason you don't want to miss any episode."

[As the series prepares for its third season] the rest of the television business will study what executives have seen so far and try to take away some lessons.

"The lesson is: there's reward in keeping an audience guessing, keeping them on their toes," Mr. Nevins said.

Mr. Littlefield said: "I think what it's telling us is that we've got to think differently when we create shows. But it also reminds us that the world we live in is both diverse and really outrageous."

LOCATION, LOCATION: THE SOPRANOS TUNES IN TO A NEW JERSEY NOBODY KNOWS (EXCEPT FOR THE MILLIONS WHO CALL IT HOME)

BY
CHARLES STRUM

Something unforeseen happened in January 1999 when a new television series became a hit: New Jersey became a star.

Not just the idea of New Jersey, or an extended riff on the jokes about New Jersey: its web of highways, nests of foundries, or pools of toxic water beside the tank farms and generating plants. The New Jersey where people live, work, and prosper finally got a fair shake.

The show is *The Sopranos* on HBO. Granted, it's about a mob boss jousting with the demons of middle age, a dark comedy with overtones of brutality. But it's also very much about a place—with moods and textures, hard and soft, inviting and repellent, silly and sophisticated. It's not about public relations. The vast green marshes of the Meadowlands also contain Dumpsters and corpses. Truck depots and abandoned waterfronts look as gritty as they are. A shimmering notion of Manhattan—a better, grander place?—is just over the horizon (Route 3 to the Lincoln, Route 4 to the G.W.B.).

But perhaps for the first time in a weekly series, New Jersey is more than just the way to someplace else, an overhead turnpike sign or a dismissive line in the script.

Suddenly, towns like Kearny, Harrison, and Belleville, rural backwaters before the Industrial Revolution, are seen as the working-class mini-metropolises they are, cramped but still vital communities of two-and-three-story houses and stores hemmed in by train tracks and old rivers.

Paramus, West Orange, Wayne, North Caldwell, Bloomfield, almost two dozen communities so far, have permitted their homes, office parks, storefronts, warehouses and restaurants to serve not just as backdrops but as themselves. You may not always know which town you're looking at, but that lawn is somebody's lawn, that house is somebody's house and, more often than not, that school or hospital or warehouse is bona fide New Jersey.

The force behind the authenticity is David Chase, the creator, writer and occasionally director of the series. He lives in Los Angeles now, but he's a Jersey guy, and he tells a cautionary tale about the first network to consider the show.

"They said, 'Oh, so you're going to fake L.A. for New Jersey?' "

" 'No,' " I said. 'I want to shoot it in New Jersey.' "

" 'Oh,' they said, 'shoot the pilot in New Jersey and then bring it back to L.A.? And do a week every five weeks back East for exteriors.' "

"They all looked at me like I was pathetic, obviously dreaming," Mr. Chase said. "It was never going to happen. In the back of my mind I sort of knew it was never going to happen."

Then he went to a meeting at HBO, and the president of original programming, Chris Albrecht, "says to me, 'So, it's going to be shot in New Jersey. You're going to get New Jersey, right?' "

"And I said, 'Absolutely. You bet.' "

"It's not that Chris loves New Jersey," Mr. Chase said, "but he wanted the show to look distinctive. He felt that if I had bothered to write it that way, it must have some meaning. He said, 'We're going to get New Jersey right,' which led us into a discussion of how the show would look." These days, movies and television series shoot for less in Canada. In recent years, Toronto has been a generic stand-in for Chicago, New York, and all suburbs in between. Mr. Chase believes that wouldn't have worked for *The Sopranos*.

"I've shot in Toronto," he said. "It isn't New

Jersey. It does look different, and that's the end of the story. There's no downtown Jersey City in Toronto. There is no collision of Hispanic, Italian, or black around an 1890s brownstone square in Toronto. These are small, unimportant details, perhaps, but not to me."

Not every scene, of course, can be shot in New Jersey. Most of the interiors are filmed at a large studio in Queens because no sound stage in New Jersey is large enough to accommodate the show's needs.

But even in Queens, Mr. Chase has laid down strict guidelines: however expedient it may be, the director is barred from sneaking across the street for a quick storefront or parking-lot shot.

"I just made it a rule," Mr. Chase said. "Let's suppose you have a half day on the stage, and then you have a scene that takes place in a field where they shoot a guy. If you have a parking lot across the street, you change the field to the lot and you don't have to move the entire company across the river. They'll tell you the waterfront looks just like the one in Newark. Baloney. Or, 'I'll show you Italian delis in Queens, and you can't tell the difference.' I'm not interested. Pretty soon that deli in Queens turns into a funeral parlor, which turns into a school, which turns into something else. No way."

Getting authentic means being efficient. That's

where the producer, Ilene Landress, and the location staff come in.

"On movies, they are usually shooting two pages a day," Ms. Landress said. "On television, it's seven or eight pages a day. We have eight days to shoot a show."

This means "breaking down the script" into scenes and locations that allow the most efficient use of cast and crew. Can a street-corner encounter, a backyard barbeque, and a schoolyard fistfight be filmed in one day?

That depends on the keen eyes of location scouts with still cameras, and the amiability of homeowners, shopkeepers, school boards, hospital administrators and various municipal overseers.

This also means hoping that potential hosts do not have what Ms. Landress called "unrealistic expectations of what they should receive."

"You hope they're starstruck," she said.

The scouts return, develop their film, and the contact sheets are distributed to Ms. Landress, Mr. Chase, the production designer, the director, and others. Then they go out and look, again.

Consider the restaurant Vesuvio, owned by Tony Soprano's high school pal Artie. Tony hears that a mob associate has been condemned to a public execution at Vesuvio, the man's favorite hangout. Tony realizes this could wreck Artie's business. He can't figure out a way to get Artie and his wife out of town during the rubout, so he does the next best thing: he asks one of his crew to torch the place.

"We needed to find a restaurant that had some space around it," Ms. Landress said, and she found the very spot in Elizabeth.

"There was a real restaurant on the corner, with a parking lot next to it," she said. "We built a little structure along the street line, with windows and a roof, and exploded that."

In another episode, a hapless debtor whom Tony runs down in a Lexus on the lawn of a Paramus office park is persuaded by Soprano pals to repay his loans by embezzling money from his company. The business meeting—a subtle use of geography—takes place on a walkway above the Great Falls, in Paterson.

To call Mr. Chase's pursuit of New Jersey loyalty, love, or sentiment would miss the point. Mr. Chase's vision for the series is rooted in something visceral about a place and the creative spirit.

He recalls an earlier experience as a producer of the detective show *The Rockford Files*.

"As great a show as it was, the thing that sort of got into my head, was that I felt *The Rockford Files* was about a place. Despite all the photography that goes on here, where Los Angeles doubles as something else, I felt that the show was happening some place real, not just in its time zone. Trailers on the beach, ritzy houses, driving into the Mexican section. That's why I took the job."

Growing up, Mr. Chase lived in Boonton, briefly, then a garden apartment in Clifton, and finally a house his father and grandfather built in North Caldwell in the late 1950s, a two-story stone-and-clapboard colonial.

"As they got established in their life, as all couples do, they sort of moved up," he said of his parents. "They built their dream house. It was based on a plan from *House Beautiful*, a house in Roslyn, L.I., which we drove out to see."

In 1968, Mr. Chase was married at St. Aloysious Roman Catholic Church, in North Caldwell, "loaded the toaster oven and other junk in the car and drove west" to work in the entertainment business. It would be an overstatement to say that New Jersey haunted him. It is simply where he's from, and it made an impression. Are the wheat fields of Kansas or the arroyos of New Mexico any more significant? Can you go home again? Wrong question. Can you forget where you grew up?

"It probably sounds corny," he said. "You never think about where you live when you're a kid. But when I got to junior high school I began to feel really lucky on some level. I knew I lived someplace special. I knew it was not like anyplace else."

Speaking of Bloomfield Avenue, the lengthy shopping district that runs through several Essex County communities, Mr. Chase said: "You could be in Iowa City or in West Virginia, it wouldn't make a difference, yet if you climb a tree, you see the New York City skyline. I lived so close to the actual throbbing center of the entire world, yet out here there were fireflies and truck farms."

These are the reminiscences of a baby boomer. Perhaps just a few years older than Tony Soprano (Mr. Chase is evasive about his own age), he is nonetheless part of the great post-war suburban advance, with a sense memory for immigrant experience of his Italian grandparents and the family's physical and emotional migration from city to single-family home on a newly paved street.

When Mr. Chase was a boy, Newark was a thriving city of factories and department stores and a vibrant clash of ethnic neighborhoods. So were Paterson, Jersey City and Elizabeth, and the smaller blue-collar towns around them.

Such a one is Kearny, about nine square miles of Hudson County, just east of the Passaic River. On one side, you can see Newark, with a magnificent view of Sacred Heart Cathedral. On the other, Jersey City and Manhattan's skyline.

In between live 35,000 people on streets of multifamily houses separated for the most part only by

driveways or alleys. The storefronts still help to identify the immigrant groups: Irish bars, Italian restaurants, Polish sausage shops and, most recently,
Portuguese bakeries.

As with much of New Jersey, Kearny was settled
by the Dutch, who bought it from the Indians. It
underwent several name changes, and was called
Harrison (now a separate town) until 1867, when it
was renamed for Maj. Gen. Philip Kearny, a Union
officer who was killed at Chantilly, VA, in 1862. Belle
Grove, the Kearny family estate that resembled a
French chateau, was a longtime landmark in the area.

What's so special about Kearny? Everything
and nothing. The history and geography lesson
would be lost on Tony Soprano or his associates.
But the texture of the place is familiar to them, to
anyone, who has come to expect realism and
authenticity.

The point is: you don't have to go to Little Italy
to have a mob sit-down.

All you need, in this case, is Satiale's, a pork
store, which occupies center stage in one episode.
Satiale's is one of the few exteriors that doesn't
really exist. It is an empty double storefront at 101
Kearny Ave., in the southern part of town. But for
one episode, it was a thriving Italian meat market,
its interior supporting columns painted the colors of
the Italian flag. Up the block is a firehouse, and next

door is the very real Irish-American Club of Kearny (founded 1933).

The other day, several older men with brogues stood beneath the Irish flag outside and graciously opened the door to their members-only clubhouse.

Inside, John Kelly, who was born in Glasgow and came to Kearny 38 years ago, was only too happy to talk about the film crew's visit next door.

"It's the one where he meets with the old Jewish guy," Mr. Kelly said, referring to an episode in which an actor dressed as a Hasidic businessman solicits Tony's aid in putting some muscle on a troublesome son-in-law. "They fixed the place up and put little tables out on the sidewalk."

So they did. A perfectly cozy corner of Kearny on a sunny day, a short walk from St. Ceclia's Roman Catholic Church and just a little farther from the thread and linen companies that brought Scottish and Irish workers here in the last quarter of the 19th century.

Mr. Kelly pointed to the two pool tables and said that they figured in another scene in which F.B.I. agents interrupt crew members and find an arsenal of guns beneath a false table top.

"I watch it every week," Mr. Kelly said enthusiastically. And he added: "Everytime they take the Irish flag down and put up the Italian flag, we get $250."

EDIE FALCO: REHABILITATING HER IMAGE

BY
GINIA BELLAFANTE

When some aspiring actresses envision their own stardom, they think of time spent writing gushy notes to their good friend Tom Ford, thanking him for all those feathered jeans and python stilettos he keeps sending over, no bill enclosed.

During the decade-plus she struggled to make it in show business, Edie Falco was never one to harbor those fantasies. Fashion simply wasn't something Ms. Falco, the star of *The Sopranos*, the HBO series, thought much about. For years she happily made do with unfeathered jeans and discarded clothes from the movies on which a friend, Eric Mendelsohn, assisted the costume designers. Once, Mr. Mendelsohn recalled, he gave Ms. Falco items from a film in which the lead character, named Dottie, just wore things with dots. "For a long time, Edie only wore dots," Mr. Mendelsohn said. Now a director, he cast Ms. Falco in the title role of his first feature, *Judy Berlin*, released in February [2000].

But this kind of ad hoc approach to dressing doesn't work once you are finally famous, as Ms. Falco is learning. Shortly after a television show declared her one of the worst-dressed guests at the Emmys in September [1999]—an event in which she won the best-actress award for her portrayal of Carmela Soprano, the mob wife with social aspirations—HBO provided Ms. Falco with the services of a stylist, Toni Fusco, and a $20,000 budget to help the actress refurbish her image.

From her apartment in Manhattan last week, Ms. Falco said she was humiliated when she discovered from friends that panelists on Melissa and Joan River's post-Emmy show had found her seemingly innocuous Pamela Dennis skirt and halter top so offensive. "It's actually a big deal for me to get dressed like a grown-up," she explained. "I thought I looked good."

"I was embarrassed at how embarrassed I was," she said.

Ms. Falco dealt with her shame by joking to all her *Sopranos* colleagues about her worst-dressed status, hoping she'd be the first to tell them. (Everyone, as it turns out, already knew.) Ms. Falco began asking a *Sopranos* costume designer for fashion advice, and soon enough Ms. Fusco was called by the network's talent-relations office to help the *Sopranos* star do some shopping. (A spokeswoman for HBO said she couldn't comment on the matter.)

"I thought she looked beautiful at the Emmys," Ms. Fusco said. "I felt so bad for her." On their major shopping outing, Ms. Fusco took the actress to DKNY (Ms. Falco's suggestion), Barney's New York, Bergdorf Goodman and Manolo Blahnik (the stylist's choices). Ms. Falco bought a pantsuit, a handkerchief skirt, some cashmere sweaters and a few pairs of pumps. But bleeding HBO dry she is not. The actress's total purchases came to about $4,000.

HE ENGINEERED A MOB HIT, AND NOW IT'S TIME TO PAY UP

BY
BILL CARTER

If there is one thing a soprano should know, it's how to pull off an encore.

But for David Chase, the maestro behind *The Sopranos*, the HBO mob opera that became the most wildly celebrated show of turn-of-the-century American television, the prospect of an encore to last season's critical and commercial triumph is bringing with it an almost crushing burden of extravagant expectations.

"I have back problems such that I can't walk," Mr. Chase said, forcing a laugh as he reeled off a litany of his recent physical woes. "I have lip problems, problems with my chest wall. I shouldn't say it's related to the pressure, but I think so. I really do."

The return of *The Sopranos* to HBO this coming Sunday night at 9 is surely the most eagerly awaited second season of a television series in recent years. The first 13 episodes last year were called everything from the best show of the year to the best of the decade to even the best television show ever. HBO has waged a promotional campaign that has underscored that praise, capitalized it, put it in italics and shouted it from the rooftops.

Brad Grey, who with Mr. Chase is an executive producer of the show, said, "You see everything HBO is doing and, to be honest, you enjoy it in one sense. But I try to remind everyone: Let's all remember, we're doing a television show here."

Mr. Chase is a veteran television writer who has worked on such series as *The Rockford Files* and *Northern Exposure*. He created *The Sopranos* from his own intensely personal vision after years of trying to sell the story of Tony Soprano, a strikingly human northern New Jersey mobster, and his dysfunctional families, personal and professional, to movies and then to television networks. He admitted he had no inkling when he wrapped up the initial batch of episodes last January that he would soon be at the center of a success so phenomenal he would begin receiving fan letters from people like Stephen King and signed guitars from Elvis Costello.

"I mean, this is beyond my wildest dreams," Mr. Chase said in an interview at the Stanhope Hotel near his home in Manhattan. "Last year we'd be out there shooting, myself and the cast, and we'd say to ourselves, 'Who's going to watch this?' We were having a really good time doing it. And I guess it's the Puritan ethic: if you're really enjoying yourself, you're going to be punished."

Instead, of course, Mr. Chase and his actors, James Gandolfini, who plays Tony; Edie Falco, who plays his wife, Carmela; Nancy Marchand, who plays his conniving mother, Livia; and many of the others were swept away in a wave of adulation, including Emmys for Mr. Chase (writing) and for Ms. Falco (leading actress in a drama series).

Now comes the hard part. Doing it again.

"When I sat down to start the second season I did have the feeling, now what am I going to do?" Mr. Chase said. "And you're aware there's a thing called a sophomore slump." The pressure, he said, began to kick in fully last April, when the show became the subject of a special event put on by the Museum of Television and Radio in Los Angeles. It was mobbed with fans from the entertainment industry.

"I could sit here and say, listen, I'm an artist, we artists do things for ourselves. It's really about expressing ourselves and pleasing ourselves," Mr. Chase said. "And there's a certain truth to that. I think you have to be somewhat true to your vision. Otherwise you'd go crazy chasing something all the time.

"But we're social animals. We're like dogs. If the other dogs turn on you, it's going to hurt. You're going to feel bad. You don't want the rest of the pack to turn on you, the pack that first embraced you. I'd be kidding you to say it was anything else."

Mr. Chase said he and his team of writers started discussions about framing a second season as far back as last February. The biggest problem they faced, he said, was purely mechanical: having closed Year One with Tony's mother having organized an attempt on his life, and the arrest of his other main antagonist, Uncle Junior, "Suddenly Tony and his mother are not speaking," Mr. Chase said. "And Uncle Junior's not there. All the things you rely on to get through a writers' meeting to be able to go home—'So then he talks to his mother and they have a fight about X'—you don't have those anymore."

There was no specific plan to write the season finale last year with some kind of dangling plot points, Mr. Chase said. "We kept thinking we didn't know there'd be a next season. We've got to shoot our best shot. We'll have to sacrifice whatever second season there is to the first, because the first is all we have. So there was some stuff to work out."

The solutions include new characters, like Tony's long-lost sister, Janice, an exile from the counterculture (whose commune name is the Hindu goddess

Parvati), and a threatening mobster just out of the pen, Richie Aprile. Mr. Chase said his biggest problem remained Tony's relationship with his mother, one reason Tony was in therapy all last season.

Not only is it difficult to find a way to bring Tony and Livia back even into the same room, he said, but, "coming off the events of last year, things happened to Tony to make him a more volatile person."

While the violence quotient, which Mr. Chase said the series had consciously tried to keep under control last season, may seem slightly elevated as the season begins, he added, "It's not that we just want to pump it up and put more violence in it, but that Tony has a lot more rage."

Tony's rage was a factor in the one instance last season when the show ran into some opposition from HBO, Mr. Chase said. In the now-memorable episode where Tony takes his daughter Meadow on a college-shopping trip to Maine and encounters a former gang member who turned state's evidence, HBO executives vocally protested its climax, where Tony kills his despised former colleague with his bare hands.

"HBO said you can't do this," Mr. Chase said. "You've built up the most interesting protagonist on television in the past 25 years, and now you're just going to lose it. There was a big discussion." He said he argued that to have Tony not kill "a rat" would be so counter to his character "that we'd lose viewers."

As it turned out, the episode was almost too good for Mr. Chase. "I saw it and said: 'Why did we do this for a TV series? This would be such a great independent movie.' "

HBO's decision to allow Tony to be seen committing brutal murder underscored Mr. Chase's conviction that *The Sopranos* could have achieved this level of success only on an outlet like HBO.

Originally, Mr. Grey, whose studio, now called Basic Entertainment, owned the right to the show, placed it at the Fox network. After a pilot script, the network passed on making the series, as did CBS and ABC. Mr. Grey says: "The truth is I was wrong. You could never have made this at Fox or any other network."

Mr. Chase said that restrictions on the wholesale vulgarity that contributes so significantly to the show's verisimilitude would have been the least of the problems at a network. "I just know they would have tried to make it that, on the side, he's helping the F.B.I. find the guys who blew up the World Trade Center. That claptrap. That would have been horrible."

Thirteen new episodes are in the final stages of production. HBO has already made it clear it wants more, and Mr. Chase said he has committed verbally to another season. "We'll start meeting again in February, blocking out stories." After that, he said, there are a "bunch of clauses" for further seasons.

"I love this," Mr. Chase said. "Who would let go of this?"

It is a big change, he admitted, after having chafed for much of his career at being limited mainly to television. "All my life I wanted to do movies. I just resented every moment I spent in television. But I would up in TV and it provided a good living and I was very fortunate that I worked on really good shows.

"But for me it was always cinema, cinema, cinema. Now this has been so good. Where am I ever going to go where it's going to be this good again?"

—January 11, 2000

AFTERWORD: ABOUT DAVID CHASE

BY
STEPHEN J. CANNELL

In the mid-seventies, I was the Writer/Producer and Co-creator of *The Rockford Files*. Our close knit staff consisted of Juanita Bartlett, Charles Johnson, and our Executive Producer, Meta Rosenberg.

Juanita and I had just completed a grueling season, where the two of us had written seventeen of the twenty-two episodes. We told Meta that we didn't think we could pull off another year like that. Meta, who was always on the prowl for new writers, told us that she had found a wonderful new talent and quickly passed around a few scripts by a little-known writer named David Chase. I read his material and, not wanting to admit too much—ego being what it is in Hollywood—I reluctantly agreed that he "showed some promise." Quickly, Juanita and I accepted David onto our writing staff.

David arrived a few mornings later and was assigned an office across the hall from mine. I remember him as slender, with a shy demeanor, offset by mischievous eyes and a dark, rapier-quick wit.

There was little chance to really get acquainted that morning, as Juanita and I were locked up, banging out scripts for the upcoming season; but that afternoon, we broke off some time to plot a story for David. It was our practice on *Rockford* to work stories in a group, but only one of us would write the actual script.

At that time, I was riding very high at the studio, having created *The Rockford Files*, as well as *Baretta* and *Black Sheep Squadron*. I thought I had the best fastball on the lot. Of course, Steve Bochco was just two buildings away, smokin' 'em over the plate. But hey, I was in my early thirties and still invested in my ego fantasies.

A week or ten days later, David turned in his first draft. So, now I have sixty pages from the "new kid," David Chase, or DeCesare; as I had come to learn, that was his off-the-boat family name.

I picked up David's work fearing the worst. After all, how could anybody but Juanita and I really capture the essence of our show, which we viewed as a tone poem for the seventies? I was fully expecting a bag of dirt as I cracked open the script.

An hour later, I had a huge dilemma.

My problem?

I thought David's script was funnier and better written than any screenplay I had done for the show in the last two seasons. How could this be happening? And worse still, how do I face this creative competition from twenty feet across the hall? Do I criticize his work? Hector this DeCesare guy, attack his confidence with the hope I might take a little spin off his curve? Or, do I go down the hall, throw my arms around him and tell him how great the damn thing really is?

Fortunately for the show, I elected the latter.

For the next three years, David became a critical part of our Writing/Producing team, providing us with some of the funniest moments and best scripts on that series.

Your writing colleagues on a show are like family. On *Rockford*, we had a matriarchal society, with Meta as our headmistress and David, Charles, Juanita and I as the siblings. David was the younger brother who could always find the twists on a theme and mine dark humor that went well beyond what I saw elsewhere on television.

The way his mind worked fascinated me. David always saw things from a unique and totally original point of view.

Two quick stories and one observation:

We were sitting around one day during the third *Rockford* season, trying to come up with a story for Juanita to write. She had been, as luck (or sexism) would have it, stuck writing about hookers for her last couple of shows. She entered my office saying, "I'll write anything except another story about a damned hooker." David and I smiled and nodded impishly and then, just to give her a little grief, I said, "I've got an idea. Listen to this: A murder; but the only clue is a soapy washcloth with the logo, 'Pimp Daddy Motel' on the corner, and then . . ."

"No hookers," she said, grinning; but she was serious. She wasn't going near another one.

All this time, David remained silent on the couch, off somewhere else (I thought). Juanita and I started hunting around for something for her to really write, when suddenly, David piped up, "Let's do it."

"Do what?" Juanita and I asked.

"A hooker. But, here's the catch," he grinned. "She'll be a hooker with a heart of gold."

"David," Juanita said, laughing. "That's the oldest cliché in film . . . and I'm not kidding. I'm not doing another story about a prostitute."

"But, what if this girl is a tragic creature," David pushed on. "She has this huge crush on Rockford, but Rockford doesn't see it . . . doesn't know she's in love with him. He sees her only as a friend. She's this very sweet person who's always helping everyone. She's going to beauty school, trying to better herself, to make her life into something, all the time asking Rockford for dumb beauty parlor career advice, hoping he'll fall for her and . . ."

. . . Rita Kapcovitch was born.

Some time after lunch, we had the story. Juanita wrote the script (beautifully) and it won an Emmy for Rita Moreno, who played the part. But for me, this was typical David Chase. I was kidding; Juanita was adamant; but it was David, who saw a way to take the oldest cliché in film and put a dark, funny twist on it so Juanita could serve it up fresh with mustard.

Many years later—in fact, just a few years ago—we were doing *The Rockford Files* reunion movies and again, I was treated to my friend David's twisty mind; which, I have come to suspect, is the only one remotely like it on the planet!

We had plotted a two-hour story for me to write. It was about a mob boss named Joseph Cortello, whose street moniker was, for some reason unknown to Rockford, "Happy."

"I don't think they call him 'Happy' because he smiles a lot," Rockford mused darkly, on page ten of my script.

We come to learn that he got that name because he is manic-depressive and would giggle from adrenaline overflow while beating people senseless . . .

which, in the course of the story, he did to Rockford, putting him in the hospital.

So, here we had a very unique mobster; one who had bipolar disease. David's idea (natch). I'm halfway through the script, and writing a scene where Rockford has been kidnapped and taken to Happy's mansion for a little interrogation and grievous bodily harm. Happy wants to know, "Why are you in my face, Rockford? Who you working for?"

I started to write the scene and I'd felt like I had written it at least half-a-dozen times before; if not on *Wiseguy* (one of my subsequent creations), then at least on one or two of my other TV series dealing with underworld heavies.

I called David on the phone. "Help, I'm stuck," I said. "I'm working on the scene where Happy is threatening Rockford at his mansion, and it's coming out flat and ordinary."

"This is our bipolar guy, right?" David asked, clicking back into the story we'd developed a few weeks before.

"Yeah."

"Okay," David said, instantly seeing a funny twist. "What if, instead of trying to threaten Rockford, he's trying to apologize to him for the first beating, but he can't find his Lithium and instead of apologizing, everything Rockford says enrages him and he ends up almost killing him for a second time?"

"Perfect!" I exclaimed.

I wrote it and it was one of the funniest scenes in the script . . . a mobster who's trying to apologize but goes berserk instead, because he can't find his Lithium. Pure David Chase.

So, that brings us to *The Sopranos*, clearly one of the most unique, groundbreaking series of this decade; a show created and produced by David Chase. This was his sole vision, his tone poem for the Millennium, as well as a salute to his New Jersey roots. He cast the actors as real people scarred by life, instead of the picture-pretty eight by ten glossies that seem to live exclusively on TV today.

He gave us, among other things, a mobster whose mother is trying to kill him for putting her in an old folks' home and a mob boss who is in analysis—no Lithium, but Prozac this time. Here, David poses the darkly funny, but very real question: What happens if your wiseguy colleagues find out you're having an emotional breakdown and are sitting in a cracked vinyl La-z-Boy twice a week, venting mob business to a head doctor?

With *The Sopranos*, we get David Chase, unfettered and in all his glory, spilling out this uncharacteristic but jewel-encrusted madness, making you laugh and cry, while at the same time, wondering at his brilliant storytelling and perfect ear for dialogue.

And now, for my one comment on TV in general . . .

I think it is a sad commentary on the last two decades of television that this man, who was well known to all the networks for almost twenty-five years, could not get his fresh, totally unique ideas past the guardians of our public airwaves (read network executives here). Instead of *The Sopranos*, we more often got mindless clones of last year's semi-hits, while David made his living running other people's shows, unable to sell his own.

Not until HBO finally saw his incredible gift did he get a chance to stand alone on a stage of his own making.

How could somebody who made me see my own weakness with his strengths, back in the seventies, have to wait almost thirty years to be treated to the success he so richly deserves?

Go figure.

Maybe there are those who would excuse it by saying he just needed those twenty-five years for seasoning.

But, I was there. I read that first *Rockford* script

and was humbled by it. So, if you want a knowledgeable opinion from somebody who knows, I say . . .

FUGEDDABOUDIT.

—January 7, 2000

PHOTO CREDITS

Page 1: Photograph of James Gandolfini at the press junket for "The Sopranos" Copyright © 2001 Armando Gallo/Retna Limited, U.S.A.

Page 35: Photograph of James Gandolfini and Edie Falco at the press junket for "The Sopranos" Copyright © 2001 Armando Gallo/Retna Limited, U.S.A.

Page 47: Photograph of Jamie Lynn Sigler and Robert Iler at Teen People and L'Oreal's "Teens Who Will Change the World," in NYC Copyright © 2000 Barry Talsenick/Retna Limited, U.S.A.

Page 57: Photograph of Lorraine Bracco at the "Inside the Sopranos" ATAS Panel Discussion in Hollywood, California Copyright © 2000 Barry Talsenick/Retna Limited, U.S.A.

Page 67: Photograph of Jamie Lynn Sigler and Jason Cerbone at the opening night party for "Cinderella" in NYC Copyright © 2001 Joe Marzullo/Retna Limited, U.S.A.

Pages 70-71: Photograph of Dominic Chianese, Edie Falco, Tony Sirico, and Vincent Pastore at the "Inside the Sopranos" ATAS Panel Discussion in Hollywood, California Copyright © 2000 Ed Geller/Retna Limited, U.S.A.

Page 75: Photograph of Edie Falco and Lorraine Bracco at the "Inside the Sopranos" ATAS Panel Discussion in Hollywood, California Copyright © 2000 Ed Geller/Retna Limited, U.S.A.

Page 89: Photograph of Vincent Pastore and Dominic Chianese at the "Inside the Sopranos" ATAS Panel Discussion in Hollywood, California Copyright © 2000 Ed Geller/Retna Limited, U.S.A.

Page 97: Photograph of "The Sopranos" creator David Chase at Manolo's restaurant in New Jersey Copyright © 1999 The New York Times/Librado Romero.

Page 107: Photograph of Aida Turturro and Robert Iler at the premiere of "61*" in NYC Copyright © 2001 John Spellman/Retna Limited, U.S.A.

Page 108: Photograph of James Gandolfini at the premiere of "Under Hellgate Bridge" in NYC Copyright © 1999 Joseph Marzullo/Retna Limited, U.S.A.

Page 114: Photograph of Edie Falco at the 53rd Annual Emmy Awards in Century City, California Copyright © 2001 Jeff Slocomb/Retna Limited, U.S.A.

Page 118: Photograph of Nancy Marchand Copyright © 1981 Lynn McAffe/Globe Photos, Inc.

Page 123: Photograph of Nancy Marchand Copyright © 2001 Barry Talesnick/Retna Limited, U.S.A.

Page 124: Photograph of Jamie Lynn Sigler at the 1st "Latina Model Search" Copyright © 2002 Darla Khazei/Retna Limited, U.S.A.

Page 128: Photograph of Rober Iler at "The Sopranos" new season premiere in NYC Copyright © 2001 John Spellman/Retna Limited, U.S.A.

Page 132: Photograph of Dominic Chianese at the premiere of "Mickey Blue Eyes" in NYC Copyright © 1999 Max Smith/Retna Limited, U.S.A.

Page 136: Photograph of Lorraine Bracco at the 2nd Annual DGA Honors Gala in NYC Copyright © 2000 Bill Davila/Retna Limited, U.S.A.

Page 140: Photograph of David Proval at the "Inside the Sopranos" ATAS Panel Discussion in Hollywood, California Copyright © 2000 Ed Geller/Retna Limited, U.S.A.

Page 144: Photograph of Aida Turturro at the All-Star Tribute to Joni Mitchell Copyright © 2000 Bill Davila/Retna Limited, U.S.A.

Page 148: Photograph of Jerry Adler at the WB Network Upfront 2001 in NYC Copyright © 2001 John Spellman/Retna Limited, U.S.A.

Page 151: Photograph of Jerry Adler at the WB Network Upfront 2001 in NYC Copyright © 2001 Walter McBride/Retna Limited, U.S.A.

Page 152: Photograph of Michael Imperioli at the press junket for "The Sopranos" Copyright © 2001 Armando Gallo/Retna Limited, U.S.A.

Page 157: Photograph of Michael Imperioli at the 12th Annual GLAAD Media Awards Copyright © 2001 Joseph Marzullo/Retna Limited, U.S.A.

Page 158: Photograph of Vincent Pastore at the premiere of "Made" in NYC Copyright © 2001 John Spellman/Retna Limited, U.S.A.

Page 162: Photograph of Steven Van Zandt at the 2nd Annual DGA Honors Gala in NYC Copyright © 2000 Bill Davila/Retna Limited, U.S.A.

Page 165: Photograph of Steven Van Zandt at the press junket for "The Sopranos" Copyright © 2001 Armando Gallo/Retna Limited, U.S.A.

Page 166: Photograph of Tony Sirico at the "Inside the Sopranos" ATAS Panel Discussion in Hollywood, California Copyright © 2000 Ed Geller/Retna Limited, U.S.A.

Page 170: Photograph of Joe Pantaliano at the 15th Annual IFP/West Inde Spirit Awards in Santa Monica, California Copyright © 2000 Ed Geller/Retna Limited, U.S.A.

Page 174: Photograph of Drea de Matteo at the "The Virgin Suicides" in NYC Copyright © 2000 John Spellman/Retna Limited, U.S.A.

Page 178: Photograph of Jason Cerbone at the premiere of "Sex and the City" in NYC Copyright © 2001 John Spellman/Retna Limited, U.S.A.

Page 182: Photograph of Annabelle Sciorra at the 1998 Gotham Awards in NYC Copyright © 2000 John Spellman/Retna Limited, U.S.A.

Page 187: Photograph of Edie Falco, David Chase, and Lorranie Bracco at the "Inside the Sopranos" ATAS Panel Discussion in Hollywood, California Copyright © 2000 Barry Talesnick/Retna Limited, U.S.A.

Page 195: Photograph of James Gandolfini at the 16th Annual Museum of Moving Image Salutes Julia Roberts in NYC Copyright © 2001 Bill Davila/Retna Limited, U.S.A.

Page 207: Photograph of Edie Falco at the press junket for "The Sopranos" Copyright © 2001 Armando Gallo/Retna Limited, U.S.A.

Page 213: Photograph of Jamie Lynn Sigler and Edie Falco at the 57th Annual Golden Globe Awards at the Beverly Hilton in CA Copyright © 2000 Steve Granitz/Retna Limited, U.S.A.

Page 223: Photograph of David Chase at the press junket for "The Sopranos" Copyright © 2001 Armando Gallo/Retna Limited, U.S.A.